Global Taxes for World Government

by Cliff Kincaid

Huntington House Publishers

Huntington House Publishers
P.O. Box 53788
Lafayette, Louisiana 70505

Library of Congress Card Catalog
Number 96-077783
ISBN 1-56384-125-8

Contents

The Second American Revolution 1

The American Revolution was sparked by a foreign power trying to tax us. Today, another foreign power—the United Nations—is actively seeking to tax us. But, unless an organized antiglobal tax resistance movement is created within U.S. borders, the U.N. and its allies will succeed in draining more wealth away from the U.S., making American citizens into mere serfs of an international bureaucracy, if not a world government.

It is fashionable to dismiss concerns about the U.N. as conspiracies and paranoid fantasies. People who regard the U.N. as any kind of threat to American sovereignty are sometimes dismissed as members of militia groups who see "black helicopters" or envision the formation of "concentration camps" to house American patriots in the event of a U.N. takeover. However, even members of Congress are increasingly viewing the U.N. as a threat.

For example, Rep. Joe Scarborough introduced a bill to get us completely out of the U.N. This was not because he was an isolationist. On the contrary, he favored a powerful international role for the U.S., directing a group of free and democratic nations against the forces of global tyranny. Scarborough simply came to the realization, brought on by fifty years of U.N. activities, that the U.N. has not served American interests and has been an impediment to the growth of human freedom and progress in the world.

Other members of Congress have spoken out strongly against U.N. global tax schemes, U.N. control of American troops, U.N. involvement in Nazi-like population control programs, and even U.N. control of our parks, as evidenced by the brazen attempt by a U.N. committee to dictate economic development near Yellowstone.

The U.N. has survived for fifty years and grown in strength and arrogance largely because of the perception that it is doing good. It's true that it has helped some refugees and children, but the prospect of paying global taxes to the U.N. will serve to enlighten many Americans about the organization's true agenda. Like King George, the U.N. regards us as unruly subjects to be enslaved or crushed if necessary.

I highlighted global tax schemes in my first book, *Global Bondage, The U.N. Plan to Rule the World.* At the time, I was struck by how liberal journalists tried to play down the significance of these international revenue-raising plans. When they were openly debated at the 1995 U.N.-sponsored World Summit for Social Development, reporters for the *Washington Post* and the *New York Times* mentioned them only in passing, in stories deep inside their respective papers. One of the cheerleaders for global tax schemes was France's Socialist then Prime Minister Francois Mitterand. His involvement was appropriate; global taxes mean socialism on a worldwide scale.

Wasn't it big news that the U.N. was considering the power to tax? Of course it was. But, these reporters, already sympathetic to the world body, recognized how explosive the news really could be. If highlighted, it would have outraged the American people—just a few months before U.N. fiftieth anniversary celebrations were scheduled—and may have created even more anti-U.N. sentiment than already existed. Plus, these journalists probably supported the schemes on the ground that the revenue would go to help "the poor." Stories about the "undertaxed" American people regularly make their way into the liberal press for the purpose of shaming us into coughing up more big bucks for government at all levels.

Working with the American Sovereignty Action Project (ASAP), Americans for Tax Reform (ATR), Accuracy in Media, and other groups, I have been working diligently to bring the issue of global taxes to national prominence. After reading this book, those interested in pursuing this matter should contact me at P.O. Box 146, Owings, Maryland, 20736.

Back in October of 1995, I was part of a press conference featuring ATR President Grover Norquist, presidential candidate Alan Keyes, and former Assistant Secretary of State John Bolton. We issued my thirty-four-page monograph, "No New Taxes? Tell the U.N." This was a reference to George Bush's famous phrase "Read my lips: No new taxes." Of course, Bush broke his word and paid the price. Taxes are always a highly charged presidential campaign issue in America, and they should be a highly charged international issue as well. American politicians should not shy away from it. The issue of global taxes is crucial to America's place in the world. We were born as a nation in a tax revolt, and perhaps we will regain our greatness in a tax revolt, this one against the U.N. and the international elites.

Yet, our October 1995 press conference failed to excite or even interest the "mainstream" press. One writer for the liberal *New Republic* ridiculed the event and me personally, saying I was the type whose writings usually ended up as letters to the editor in obscure publications. It was a big laugh for him.

But then, in early 1996, they stopped laughing. This is when United Nations Secretary General Boutros Boutros-Ghali, in an interview with the BBC in January 1996, himself openly advocated a "light international tax" to pay for U.N. operations. The concept of a "light" tax was the funny line. But, at least he called it a tax and not a *revenue enhancer*, the term used by some American politicians.

In this interview Boutros-Ghali said this taxing power would provide the U.N. with "independence." In the U.N. version of "free at last," he said, "I will not be under the daily financial will of the Member States." Asked if he thought he would succeed in getting the power to tax, he replied, "It takes time. I am sure that we will win in the end and that we will obtain from the international community [recognition] that we need to have our own income."

In the same month, in a lecture at the University of Oxford, England, Boutros-Ghali went into more detail. In order for the U.N. to "operate on a secure and steady independent financial foundation," he proposed "measures for consideration," including a "fee on speculative international financial transactions, a levy on fossil fuel use (or its resulting pollution); earmarking a small portion of the anticipated decline in world military expenditures, utilizing some resources released by the elimination of unnecessary subsidies; resources generated by a stamp tax on international travel and travel documents, or a levy on global currency transactions."

Boutros-Ghali added that "finding the right formula will be a project of vast importance for the future of the international community. It will be the role of the Secretary General to bring this project to successful fruition in the twenty first century."

Boutros-Ghali confirmed the dangers I described in my 1995 book, *Global Bondage, The U.N. Plan to Rule the World*, and my ATR monograph. This time it didn't take long for American policymakers to react. Senators Bob Dole, Jesse Helms, and Judd Gregg called for a General Accounting Office (GAO) investigation of how far along these plans were. They introduced legislation to cut off all funds to the U.N. if such a tax were ever implemented. This was all well and good, except that I had basically put together all of this information for ATR. What was needed was immediate congressional hearings.

The reaction of the Clinton administration was fascinating. The U.S. Department of State issued a statement through spokesman Nicholas Burns that was headlined "U.S. Opposition to Worldwide Tax to Support the U.N." It said,

> A January 14 interview of the United Nations Secretary General with the BBC in London has attracted attention to proposals for new means of raising funds to support the work of the United Nations. The United Nations does not have the authority to impose or collect any form of tax, and the U.S. Government would

not consent to any proposal to grant it such authority.

The United States continues to believe that the best way to ensure adequate and predictable funding for the United Nations system is through reforms which result in a fair system of financing, and which reduce overall costs and allow reinvestments of savings in areas of high priority to member states. An approach to fundraising that involved any form of international tax would be inconsistent with the intergovernmental nature of the organization and could undermine the sovereignty of member states.[1]

This would appear to end all discussion, were it not for the fact that the State Department response was completely misleading. However, the statement was important because of what it says about the political nature of this explosive issue. The Clinton administration thought it was suicidal to publicly embrace global taxes. However, the truth was that one of its top appointees to the U.N. had done just that.

Though it has been kept hidden from most Americans, the U.N. and its supporters have been planning a series of international taxes for many years, and Clinton officials were part of this scheming. Through a key appointee at the U.N. Development Program (UNDP), James Gustave Speth, the Clinton administration privately supported the idea of international taxes, while publicly the State Department was claiming they were a bad idea. The UNDP is the U.N. agency that openly promoted world government and global taxes in its 1994 "Human Development Report." Speth's name was on the report, and he publicly endorsed global taxes at a UNDP news conference. At the 1995 World Summit for Social Development, the UNDP staged events designed to move these schemes along toward implementation.

How could the Clinton administration maintain it would not consent to global taxes when one of its own people at the U.N. was leading the charge for them? Unfortunately, this was typical of the Clinton administration's approach to many matters—saying one thing, doing another. In short, they lied. And, the media let Clinton officials get away with it.

In a story in the *Washington Post*, however, John M. Goshko admitted that ideas for global taxes have "been kicking around for years and are well known to anyone familiar with U.N. affairs." This was news to readers of the *Post* because the newspaper had failed to inform them. One day later, the *Post*'s editorial page weighed in on the subject, calling it "funny" that anyone would believe the U.N. wanted global taxes for world government. It said, "The notion of the United Nations as a would-be world government chewing up the sovereignty of state dies hard." It said Boutros-Ghali "deserves to be criticized for daydreaming."

In one case, however, the *Post* came clean. Jessica Mathews, a senior fellow at the Council on Foreign Relations and a regular columnist for the *Post*, jumped aboard the global tax bandwagon, declaring that "nearly every expert look at U.N. financing has recommended a source of nongovernmental funds (e.g., by taxing air travel, currency exchange, etc.)." Her comments, however, were confusing. How a tax translates into "nongovernmental funds" is mindboggling, and these "experts" mostly turn out to be current or former U.N.

bureaucrats. The "nongovernmental funds" actually mean that the U.N., acting like a world government, would collect the funds.

But, the notion that a global tax requires U.S. "consent"—through a treaty—is not necessarily true. The U.N. charter is somewhat vague about how the organization is to be financed. Article 17 simply says that the General Assembly should consider and approve the budget of the organization and that the expenses "shall be borne by the Members as apportioned by the General Assembly." There is nothing in here ruling out global taxes.

Moreover, the third part of article 17 says that the General Assembly "shall consider and approve any financial and budgetary arrangements with specialized agencies." This is a major loophole that enables international agencies to hide the sources of their financing. An example of such an arrangement is the Global Environmental Facility, composed of the U.N. Development Program, the World Bank, and the United Nations Environment Program.

Furthermore, article 29 of the U.N. charter contains another major loophole, saying that "the Security Council may establish such subsidiary organs as it deems necessary for the performance of its functions." Under this provision a special war crimes tribunal was created, an unprecedented development. It is not inconceivable that these "subsidiary organs" could be financial in nature and could be tax-raising entities.

It's true that a tax-raising treaty could be drafted and submitted to the U.S. Senate for ratification. However, this itself presents a constitutional problem since the U.S. Constitution says that tax-raising bills have to originate in the U.S. House of Representatives. So, how could they push something like this through without trashing our founding document?

Yet another U.N. treaty, the United Nations Convention to Combat Desertification (CCD), indicates how they might strike. Rather than draft and submit treaties that lack funding, they will put forward treaties that have financial mechanisms built into them, forcing member states to cough up the money to various U.N.-affiliated agencies.

This treaty, literally designed to save drylands (as opposed to wetlands), contains a provision, article 21, dealing with "financial mechanisms." It says that the "Conference of the Parties," comprised of those nations signing the document, shall "facilitate the provision of necessary funding at the national, subregional, regional and global levels for activities pursuant to relevant provisions of the Convention." This reference to funding on "global levels" is obviously a foot-in-the-door to international lobbying for international revenues and more pressure for global taxes to implement the document.

In another part of the document, "Financial Resources," a reference is made to obtaining funding from the aforementioned Global Environmental Facility (GEF). Thus, a country such as the U.S. could provide funds to the GEF, which could then be channeled to those implementing the desert protection treaty. This convoluted arrangement is perfectly appropriate if one is trying to hide the real sources of funding from those who provide most of the money— that is, the American taxpayers.

Some may say that the bottom line is that, regardless of what the U.N. currently says or does, the U.S. Congress must still appropriate whatever money the administration offers to "contribute." In other words, we're protected; they'll never pull it off. This ignores the dynamics of how a global tax scheme could be quietly implemented.

In a clever ploy, Sen. Jeff Bingaman (D-NM) in 1995 introduced a variation of a global tax to fund liberal initiatives. Bingaman, the head of a working group of senators, prepared the proposal at the request of Senate Democratic Leader Tom Daschle. He didn't call it a global tax, but his proposal did call for an "A-Fund," financed by a "securities transfer excise tax" (STET) to be enforced on an international basis by the G-7 industrialized countries. The Group of Seven countries is the U.S., Canada, France, Germany, Italy, Japan, and Britain. The A-Fund, which stands for Financial Markets Allied with America's Businesses and Working Families Fund, was supposed to be one Democratic answer to the issue of job insecurity.

Introduced as one part of a fifty-seven-page 28 February report, "Scrambling to Pay the Bills: Building Allies for America's Working Families," Bingaman wanted a "less-than-one-half-of-one-percent and declining tax" on security sales. By his calculations, it could bring in anywhere from $27 billion to $62 billion a year. However, it is clear that the tax is not limited to those rich speculators who supposedly have disrupted the financial markets.

The report explained:

> Our proposal would impose a small and diminishing securities transfer excise tax (STET) on broad-based security sales made less than two years after purchase. The tax would extend to transactions by individuals, corporations, and

tax-exempt pension funds and other entities and would apply to stocks, bonds, options, futures, and swaps of currency, interest rates, and other assets. This would include trades on behalf of Americans and American assets on American and foreign exchanges, whether done directly or through any intermediary investment fund.

In other words, ordinary Americans with investments in pension funds, the stock market, and IRAs would pay the financial price.

Some other countries, the report claimed, have already imposed "some form" of securities transaction tax. In this case, however, it would have to be global. "To minimize any evasion of the tax in global financial markets, the U.S. should take the lead in the G-7 to coordinate a policy preventing STET evasion," the Bingaman report explained. This effort to "coordinate a policy" is obviously the beginnings of the effort to implement the tax.

The decision to go to the G-7 for support is significant. Studies endorsing global taxes have been underwritten by several G-7 countries, including the governments of Germany, Japan, and Canada. As noted, France, under its Socialist then Prime Minister Francois Mitterand, was a big booster of global taxes at the 1995 U.N.-sponsored World Summit for Social Development.

In addition, Russia can be counted on to join the campaign. Yuli Vorontsov, the Russian ambassador to the U.S. and an adviser to President Boris Yeltsin, was a member of the Commission on Global Governance, a group which produced a 1995 report, "Our Global Neighborhood," advocating a series of international taxes.

To protect themselves against charges that they are proposing a global tax to bail the U.N. out of its financial difficulties, the Senate Democrats would correctly point out that they want the revenue from this STET to go for such things as financing tax deductions for higher education, tax credits for children, workforce training, the "school to work" program, and the notorious Goals 2000 educational plan. Some of the revenue would also go for "government-industry partnerships" and government export promotion programs.

But, what is to prevent such a tax, once it is established, from generating revenues for international bodies like the U.N., the World Bank, or the International Monetary Fund? Isn't this a logical next step, especially with the U.N. crying poverty and threatening bankruptcy?

It is perhaps more than coincidental that leftist British journalist Martin Walker, writing about the benefits of global taxation in *World Policy Journal* back in 1993, suggested implementing an international tax by first going through the G-7, the same approach as the Senate Democrats.

"The trick, of course, is in achieving international consensus" for global taxes, Walker said. "No individual government or trading center dares impose a unilateral tax on its own share of the constant global flow. Any that did would instantly find the business being shifted to more hospitable climes. But an agreement by the dominant G-7 economies, backed by the OECD [Organization for Economic Cooperation and Development], requiring their own banks and trading houses to comply, should suffice to police such a relatively painless system of exploiting this global resource."

The "system," Walker said, would work this way:

> Technically, such a tax would be remarkably easy to collect through the computer systems that record each trade. It would require every bank and finance house active in the global currency markets (and they are already regulated and licensed) to open a separate U.N. bank account to which the tax would automatically be transferred when each new transaction is made.

The claim that the Bingaman proposal, or even a global tax, would never go through ignores the dynamics of how government grows under Democrats and Republicans. Despite the Republican reaction against global taxes, the truth is that, regardless of which administration is in power in Washington, D.C., the U.N. and its affiliated institutions will continue trying to extract more dollars from American taxpayers and businesses. This is because U.N. bureaucrats believe they do not have to answer to member-states of the U.N.

We are always in danger as long as we are a member of the U.N. and as long as the U.N. exists. Cuts in U.N. funding or vague promises of "reform" will not alter this equation.

Like King George more than two hundred years ago, the U.N. bureaucrats believe they're capable of ruling the world and managing our lives for us. In fact, a range of international agencies and bureaucracies already manage the affairs of the world to a remarkable degree. The U.N. is only the most visible of them. Others include the International Monetary Fund, the World Bank, and the World Trade Organization. These groups, which are part of the "U.N.

System," attempt to dictate the economic affairs of member-states, fix the value of currencies, and manage trade relationships.

In order to understand the predicament we're in today, for the purpose of recognizing the threat posed by global taxes, it is important to go back in history to the time of the American Revolution. We have to understand our founding as a nation so that the U.N. threat can be put in context. America was founded by tax resisters, and tax resistance is the key to rolling back the power of the international agencies that threaten the American way of life.

Taxes, of course, are much more than money that is paid to government. The issue is not that Americans resent paying taxes for legitimate functions of government. The issue is what these taxes represent— a transfer of control over our lives to distant bureaucrats.

Those promoting international taxes have to realize that they push their schemes at their own peril. History did not treat the British oppressors kindly, and the international elites bent on imposing global taxes on American citizens and American businesses will probably not fare well either. If the issue is well understood and not concealed from them, there is simply no question that the American people will not permit a foreign power or entity to tax them. They are certain to rise up in revolt.

It's difficult to understate the situation: we are entering a revolutionary period which may decide whether the American nation-state will survive or else be subsumed into a "global economy" in which America's elected officials act as mere colonists, recognizing a political authority above and beyond them.

The outcome hinges on whether the truth about the global tax agenda can be provided to enough people in time.

The American colonists started feeling the heavy hand of King George in 1764, when the Sugar Act was passed by the British Parliament, placing tariffs on sugar, coffee, wines, and other products imported into America. Revolutionary firebrand James Otis led the opposition, declaring, "No taxation without representation," a reference to the lack of American representation in Parliament. The tax was designed to raise money for England to pay off a war debt.

But, the antitax resistance didn't really take off until the British Parliament passed a second tax, the Stamp Act of 1765, which imposed tariffs on printed matter, including newspapers and legal documents, in the colonies. The Stamp Act was specifically designed not to regulate trade but to raise revenue, a direct tax. British Treasury official Thomas Whately described it as "a great measure . . . on account of the important point it establishes, the right of Parliament to lay an internal tax on the colonies."[2] This sounds like the U.N. today.

In the face of British power, the Sons of Liberty were born, a name given to the revolutionary colonists. Unrest, riots, and general violence greeted King George's tax-raising schemes. The homes of British sympathizers in the colonies were attacked and ransacked. Economic boycotts of British goods were launched.

The Stamp Act was repealed, but by then it was too late for the British. They were already viewed as oppressors whose intent was to destroy the American experiment. In America, forces were gathering that most of the London politicians were too smug or superior to acknowledge.

The British Parliament tried another tax, the Townshend Acts, provoking another boycott of British goods. This time, in a show of force, the British sent in troops, who also ended up competing for jobs with the colonists. Fights broke out, leading to the Boston Massacre of five colonists. The famous Boston Tea Party, a protest against a British attempt to monopolize the tea business, followed. King George said, "The colonies must either submit or triumph." The rest, as they say, is history.

It was an historic battle: the American patriots faced unfair laws, taxes, and the display of British troops on American soil. Americans had no say in what Parliament decided for the colonies because they didn't have a single representative in the British Parliament. But, they stood up to a foreign power, waged a bloody and fierce battle, and won American independence.

This situation is comparable to what the U.N. represents today, even though we pay one-third of the bills and supposedly have veto power at the world body. The problem is that a succession of administrations, Democratic and Republican, have favored the expansion of global power at the expense of American sovereignty, and we have a Congress which doesn't yet understand the dimensions of the threat.

The terms *smug* and *superior* used against the British accurately describe the international bureaucrats who are scheming right now to extract more dollars from hard-working taxpayers. Like King George, their attitude is that the Americans must submit. But, they're not the only global tax advocates. They have the support of Americans active in the environmental, pro-abortion, and antinational defense movements who want the United Nations to have the power and authority to remake the world. They want global taxes for global environmentalism, population control and reduction, and military "peacekeeping." These U.S. domestic groups are comparable to the British sympathizers of more than two hundred years ago.

What these forces are really proposing is a version of a global IRS. In fact, after learning of the U.N.'s tax plans, Sen. Robert Dole declared in a press release that it appeared as though Boutros-Ghali "wants to head up an international Internal Revenue Service."

How could global taxes evolve into a global IRS? Americans can make their own assessment based on how tax collection has evolved in the U.S. In the beginning of the American republic, there was no direct taxation. The Founding Fathers favored a system of indirect taxes, collected through excises, imposts, and duties. In the Constitution, the founders described in article I, section 9, clause 4, how a direct tax could be laid for a specific purpose—to reduce the deficit. These direct taxes would be passed through the states to the citizens but were to be proportional to the number of representatives that each state had in Congress.

As Edward A. Ellison, Jr., and John William Kurowski document in their book, *Prosperity Restored by the State Rate Tax Plan*, the first direct tax was imposed by Congress to extinguish part of the Revolutionary War debt. The direct tax was also used to extinguish part of the debt suffered during the War of 1812 and also the Civil War debt.[3]

With the passage of the Sixteenth Amendment to the Constitution in 1913, a federal income tax was

passed, and the federal government achieved the power
to determine each person's income, requiring each
person to produce all kinds of information and docu-
mentation on his or her financial life. The National
Commission on Economic Growth and Tax Reform
issued a report that described the IRS today in these
terms: "Twice as big as the CIA and five times the
size of the FBI, the IRS controls more information
about individual Americans than any other agency.
Without a search warrant, the IRS has the right to
search the property and financial documents of American citizens. Without a trial, the IRS has the right to
seize property from Americans."

In an editorial noting that the "tax army" that
extracts dollars from American taxpayers is larger than
the U.S. Army which defends them, the *Columbus
Dispatch* noted:

> The federal tax code is incredibly complex. Ac-
> cording to economists' estimates in the *Na-
> tional Tax Journal*, administering the federal
> income tax costs as least $70 billion a year, and
> some estimate the true cost as being three times
> higher.

> Each year, about 8 billion hours are spent fill-
> ing out federal income tax forms. That's the
> equivalent of 1.5 million full-time workers.

> A veritable army of accountants, tax attorneys,
> tax preparers and IRS employees is needed to
> keep Uncle Sam nourished. If one adds up half
> the accountants in the country, one-fourth of
> the lawyers and all the IRS employees, the total
> is about 1.2 million. That's triple the number
> in 1960.[4]

In *American Heritage* magazine, John Steele Gordon wrote,

> The United States Internal Revenue Code takes up six inches of shelf space in two fat volumes. But that is not the half of it. Federal tax regulations, the Talmud, if you will, to the Torah of the tax code, takes up an additional foot of shelf space in eight volumes. Thousands of accountants and lawyers devote entire careers just to small portions of this behemoth, and no one could possibly know its entirety, not even the Internal Revenue Service. Indeed, it is estimated that one-third of the inquiries made to the IRS's own 800 help line are answered incorrectly.

The impact on traditional families—America's strength—has been devastating. According to the Heritage Foundation,

> Federal taxation of families with children has increased dramatically over the past four decades. In 1948, the typical family of four paid just 3 percent of its income to the federal government in direct taxes. In 1994, the equivalent family paid 24.5 percent of its income to the federal government. . . . [W]hen state and local and indirect federal taxes are included, the tax burden on that family equals 37.6 percent of its income.

In retrospect, James Otis's phrase, "no taxation without representation," was not the answer to our problems. Our current predicament was summarized by Gerald Barzan in the words: "Taxation with representation ain't so hot either." In 1996, the average

American worked until May to pay taxes to various levels of government. Each year "Tax Freedom Day" moves later into the calender. Bowing to growing antitax sentiment, the U.S. government promises to make "tax reform" a major issue.

But, the "reform" will not be complete if international agencies continue in their dogged pursuit of the power to tax. Today, we face the prospect of being taxed by people we didn't even elect. Defenders of the U.N. might say that their proposals only amount to indirect taxes. However, in the same way the U.S. national government developed an income tax, it is entirely conceivable that the U.N. would do the same. In fact, some U.N. proponents are already calling for much broader taxes and the police powers to collect them. In the book, *The United Nations at the Crossroads of Reform*, Wendell Gordon writes:

> To begin with, the United Nations should have at least two major sources of revenue: a percentage, perhaps 25 or 30 percent, of each country's military budget . . . and a corporate (or business) income tax.
>
> It is important that a significant part of the revenue of the UN be collected directly from corporations active internationally in the form of a corporate income tax and that the UN have the police power to make such collections effective.[5]

It seems clear that the only way we are going to roll back this global tax agenda is by appealing to the revolutionary spirit, the antitax fervor that broke our ties to England more than two hundred years ago.

We have a big job ahead of us: we have to convince Americans that the economic insecurity they feel in their own lives is linked to a global agenda, whereby international institutions are consciously lowering the American standard of living and looting our national wealth. The game is an old one: the rest of the world is jealous of America, of her wealth and power. Liberals feel guilty over our historical high standard of living. Their objective is not only to redistribute our wealth here at home, but to redistribute it abroad through foreign aid programs, subsidies to international agencies, and international taxes.

The other side has a very sophisticated plan to convince people that we should look forward to paying global taxes and being global citizens. The March 1996 issue of the *Atlantic Monthly* had a fascinating cover story, "The Source of Our Discontent," exploring the fact that "many Americans fear we are losing control of the forces that govern our lives." The author, Michael J. Sandel, is a professor of government at Harvard University, one of our most prestigious institutions of higher learning. He talked about such things as the "insecurity of jobs in the global economy" and the power of giant corporations. These are very legitimate fears and problems. But, his solution took the form of advocating Big Government at the global level, saying we need "political institutions capable of governing the global economy."

Politics, he said, "must assume transnational, even global, forms," adding that "the way to respond to a global economy is to strengthen global governance and cultivate a corresponding sense of global or cosmopolitan citizenship."

Sandel explained, "Internationally minded reformers have already begun to articulate this impulse. The Commission on Global Governance . . . published a report calling for greater authority for international institutions." Indeed it did. It called for a series of global taxes to pay for world government.

If a professor of government is talking about the value of "global governance," you can be sure that many other liberal academics are true believers as well and that the notion of "global citizenship" is being drummed into impressionable young people. In one sense, this is perfectly understandable. Many young people today don't have anything to believe in. They have lost purpose and direction. From the point of view of the multinational elites, this presents a perfect opportunity for them to be molded into students who take the "cosmopolitan" view.

In order for the next generation to be conditioned into accepting world government and "global citizenship," young Americans must have their knowledge of U.S. history obliterated. The process is well underway. A federally-funded report of the National Assessment of Educational Progress revealed that nearly six in ten high school seniors lack even a basic understanding of American history. Only about 60 percent of high-school seniors could define the Monroe Doctrine, and less than half of them understood that the containment of communism was the professed goal of American policy after World War II. The results also showed that only 40 percent of all fourth-graders knew why the Pilgrims came to America. Only 7 percent could explain what was happening in Philadelphia in 1776.

In other words, Americans—and especially our children—have lost contact with our roots. In order to recapture the spirit of American independence, we have to understand where we came from. I recommend intensive studies into authentic American history and genealogical research into family histories. Most of us can trace our roots to the American Revolution and beyond. One of the early Kincaids, John Kincaid, came from Stirlingshire, Scotland, to America about the year 1684. Many Kincaids fought in the war of the revolution.

Unless we act quickly, the situation for the next generation could get even worse in the years ahead.

At the same time, allies of the U.N. are peddling a series of polls designed to convince people that global taxes are necessary and supported by large numbers of people. Polls can be designed to say whatever the questioners want them to say. But, these polls will undoubtedly continue receiving substantial media attention.

The prestigious-sounding Americans Talk Issues Foundation issued a series of surveys in 1995 claiming 75 to 79 percent of people surveyed favored a "worldwide tax on international currency trades." Asked if the U.N. should be allowed to monitor and tax international arms sales, the survey found that more than two-thirds (72 percent) would support such a plan.

But, here's the rub: the respondents to the first question were told the money would be used "to clean up the world's polluted drinking water supplies, reverse the destruction of the world's forests, and/or give a basic education to the world's children." The respondents to the second question were told the money would go for famine relief and humanitarian aid.

In other words, the survey was stacked. One can imagine what the results might be if people were asked, Would you pay global taxes to support an international bureaucracy already rife with corruption, waste, fraud, and abuse?

There is stench surrounding this organization. The president of the Americans Talk Issues Foundation is Alan Kay, who turned out to be one of the key players at the U.N.'s World Summit for Social Development in Copenhagen, Denmark. Speaking at a pro-U.N. event, Kay talked about the push for global taxes, including the participation of then-French President Mitterand and the UNDP:

> At Copenhagen, six heads of state, including Mitterand, mentioned when they came on . . . that there should be some consideration of international currency regulation or taxation. . . . What we did at Copenhagen . . . was the civil society raised the awareness, with the cooperation of UNDP and others in the U.N. . . . [We] ran a press briefing on this issue in the context of the larger issue of funding the United Nations.[6]

This is the kind of intensive effort and propaganda we are facing today. Academics, pollsters, and others will be building up public "support" for global government and global taxes.

The key is to educate the American people, especially the politicians on Capitol Hill. Though politicians of both parties talk about the need for economic growth and jobs, they seem not to grasp the fact that the world view which has made America great—the belief that scientific advancement, technology, and industrial growth leads to progress, within the context of traditional moral values—is under unprecedented assault by a wide range of domestic and international forces which masquerade under the vague term of constituting the "global economy."

Bluntly put, a massive restructuring of our economic, social, and political system is taking place. In the old days, it would have been called socialism or Marxism. Today, it's called environmental protection, sustainable development, and preserving biodiversity—all of them nice-sounding terms used by the U.N. The challenge is how we can educate the American people about what is taking place, why, and what can be done—before it is too late or before more drastic measures are required to save our country.

The challenge is a daunting one. In this battle, the American people are up against extraordinary financial resources—those of government, industry, and the big foundations. The organizations pushing global taxes include the Commission on Global Governance, Worldwatch Institute, World Resources Institute, Oxfam, the Ford Foundation, the MacArthur Foundation, Carnegie Corporation, World Federalist Association, and the Independent Commission on Population and Quality of Life.

The Commission on Global Governance was itself funded by the Netherlands, Norway, Sweden, Canada, Denmark, India, Indonesia, and Switzerland. One of the U.S. members of the commission was Adele Simmons of the megarich MacArthur Foundation.

But, big business is also a big part of the problem, even though they are being targeted as a major source of global tax revenue. The corporate members of the Business Council for the U.N. read like a "Who's Who" of the international business community. Corporate backing of the environmentalist movement was selected by Operation Spike as one of the most under-reported and covered-up stories of 1995. Overall, the Capitol Research Center finds that liberal groups receive more than three times the corporate funding of conservative groups, but it's the conservative groups which get labeled as "corporate-backed."

Consider just one of these groups, the World Resources Institute (WRI). Besides funding from many big businesses, a report by the Capitol Research Center discloses that WRI was created largely by the MacArthur Foundation in 1982 with grants totalling over $25 million by 1986 and with loans amounting to approximately $12.5 million. The report notes that, in typical revolving door fashion, then-WRI President James Gustave Speth, a founder of the Natural Resources Defense Council in 1970, later served as chairman of the Council for Environmental Quality during the Carter administration.

But, the revolving door took an international turn when Speth became the administrator of the U.N. Development Program in the Clinton administration, where he took the lead in promoting international taxes, and the White House covered for him.

Endnotes

1. Statement by Nicholas Burns, spokesman, U.S. Department of State, Office of the Spokesman, 19 January 1996.

2. M. Stanton Evans, *The Theme Is Freedom* (Washington, D.C.: Regnery Publishing, Inc., 1994), 218.

3. Edward A. Ellison., Jr., J.D., and John William Kurowski, *Prosperity Restored by the State Rate Tax Plan* (1985).

4. "Tax Army Marches On," *Columbus Dispatch*, 1 January 1996.

5. Wendell Gordon, *The United Nations at the Crossroads of Reform* (New York: M.E. Sharpe, 1994), 218.

6. Alan F. Kay, "The Need for Taming the Global Capital Markets and Developing New Means of Funding the United Nations," audio tape, recorded 31 August 1995.

Domestic Taxes for the U.N.

2

In the fight for American independence, America was the recipient of what some might call foreign aid. Critical support was secretly provided to us by France. Today, many Americans view America's destiny as helping others to fight tyranny and gaining freedom through establishing a system of self-government by which human rights are recognized as coming from God, not government.

It was in this context that President Reagan's administration provided assistance to the freedom fighters in Nicaragua and Afghanistan, turning the tide against Soviet-style communism worldwide. This mostly covert assistance was provided in the spirit of America's battle for liberty. But, "foreign aid," as the term is used these days, refers to something else entirely—grants and handouts to international organizations such as the U.N. and foreign governments. In other words, global welfare. It has nothing to do with promoting American interests or human freedom.

According to Senate report 104-99 of the Foreign Relations Committee, over the last fifty years the American people have already handed out $450 billion in foreign aid (not adjusted for inflation). But, the report quickly adds that "since foreign aid has been financed by borrowing, and interest payments have also been financed by borrowing, the actual cost of foreign aid to the U.S. according to a Congressional Research Service study, is nearly $2 trillion dollars (not adjusting for inflation)."

Ironically, those countries which have been cut-off from this kind of foreign aid—the Republic of China on Taiwan and Chile—are the ones which have grown into prosperous democratic countries. There is a lesson here. Taiwan was cut-off from the "international community" because Communist China improperly took its permanent seat on the U.N. Security Council. Chile was ostracized because it had an anti-Communist military government.

The liberals claim that foreign aid, including funding of the U.N., is an incredibly small portion of the overall federal budget. For example, "international affairs spending" of "just" $17.1 billion was proposed for fiscal year 1997.

Assuming, for a moment, that this figure is accurate, what are we getting for the money? A May 1996 Heritage Foundation study found that nearly two-thirds of the countries that receive U.S. foreign aid voted against the U.S. a majority of the time in the U.N. These countries included Haiti, whose rulers were installed by a U.S.-U.N. military operation, and Mexico, which benefited from an economic bailout largely funded by American taxpayers. Heritage Foundation analyst Bryan Johnson asked, "Why is the United States spending so much money on countries that obviously care little about America's interests abroad?"

The answer is that the purpose of the aid is not necessarily to further American interests. On the contrary, the purpose of foreign aid is to make countries dependent on federal agencies and international institutions working in tandem for the purpose of controlling their peoples and development. Foreign aid represents political control. In the same way that people enjoy welfare, U.N. bureaucrats and foreign heads of state like the arrangement because the money supports their luxurious lifestyles and enables them to control the fate of nations. The votes cast by these countries just don't seem to matter much in the overall scheme of things.

Consider what is happening in Bosnia, where a "peace deal" was achieved in 1995. A last-minute letter from World Bank President James Wolfensohn offering "reconstruction" aid for the country is what clinched the peace deal between Bosnia, Croatia, and Serbia. What was hailed as a "great foreign policy triumph" by the Clinton administration amounted to a bribe—and the American taxpayers are still getting fleeced.

The letter, dated 19 November 1995, was delivered to Bosnian President Alija Izetbegovic as the peace talks appeared to be stalling. "As the process of making peace in Bosnia and Herzegovina progresses," the letter said, "increasing attention is being focused on economic reconstruction." Wolfensohn, an appointee and close friend of President Clinton, explained to the Bosnian president that "with this letter I would like to assure you that we at the World Bank will do all we can to facilitate the financial aspects of a peace agreement to which the parties may agree," including a "major contribution" for "your most urgent economic needs."

It would be nice to think that the parties came to this agreement out of the goodness of their hearts. But, the facts of economic life on the international scene bear some close scrutiny. It turned out that Bosnia owed $450 million to the World Bank and $37 million to the International Monetary Fund (IMF). This is the share of the debt of the former Yugoslavia that Bosnia inherited when it broke away as a separate state.

Speaking at a multinational conference on 9 December 1995 in London, Wolfensohn put a price tag on the Bosnia reconstruction effort at $4.9 billion over three years, more than enough to enable Bosnia to pay off its debt. Some experts have now put the cost at four or five times that. Congress is simply handed the bill and pays.

How is it possible to make sure that Bosnia pays? Article VII of the Bosnian Constitution, written by the Clinton State Department and made a part of the treaty, mandates that the first governor of Bosnia's Central Bank be appointed through consultation with the IMF. Not surprisingly, the executive board of the IMF on 20 December 1995 admitted Bosnia as a member and immediately approved about $45 million for Bosnia. An IMF press release stated that the country's $37 million debt to the IMF was wiped out by a short-term loan provided by the Netherlands Central Bank, which was repaid from credit provided by the IMF.

The attempt in Bosnia was to create the U.N.'s first "puppet state," an unprecedented event in human history. It is doubtful that the settlement will last, but a lot of money will be lost in the process. According to the Heritage study cited earlier, Bosnia already votes against the U.S. 33 percent of the time at the U.N. If history is any guide, this percentage will rise as our aid to them increases.

The Bosnia case demonstrates that the official figure of $17 billion on "international affairs" is grossly misleading. It doesn't take into account the escalating costs of aid to Bosnia or, for that matter, the ongoing $40 billion economic bailout of Mexico largely funded by U.S. taxpayers and arranged through the IMF.

For the World Bank alone, the Heritage Foundation estimates that the U.S. has provided some $53 billion since 1944. Yet, the think tank says that, of the sixty-six less developed countries receiving money from the World Bank for more than twenty-five years, thirty-seven are no better off today than they were before they received such loans. Of these thirty-seven, most are poorer today than they were before receiving aid from the bank.

For the U.N. alone, it is estimated that $100 billion has been provided by American taxpayers over the last fifty years. Yet, now the U.N. is crying for global taxes.

At the U.N. itself, despite much talk about going broke, the bureaucrats are living high off the hog. Doing better than the U.S. president, Secretary General Boutros Boutros-Ghali had a gross salary in 1996 of $280,075 plus $25,000 for entertainment, bringing him up to an annual salary of $307,075. His annual retirement benefit is $96,616, payable after only five years on the job.

The U.N. pension and retirement fund is also doing very well. In fact, it may be the best-managed program at the U.N.—for obvious reasons. According to information provided to me, as of February 1996 it had a market value of approximately $15 billion. The U.N., which says it employs fifty thousand people worldwide, also says there are some sixty-four thousand "active fund participants" and that benefits are flowing to thirty-eight thousand people in 181 countries. It is unclear why the number of employees conflicts with the number of "active fund participants." In any case, this group provides a powerful incentive to keep the U.N. going and growing.

Officially, according to the Heritage Foundation, the U.S. provides 25 percent of the U.N. administrative budget, which funds all U.N. secretariat staff and programs. This amounted to $298 million in 1994. The U.S. share of the U.N. peacekeeping budget was 31.7 percent or $1.2 billion. On top of that, the U.S. contributes separately to U.N. specialized agencies such as the World Health Organization. In 1994, this was estimated at another $368 million. This brings the U.S.'s yearly contribution up to almost $2 billion.

But, this figure ignores the tens of billions that have been improperly taken out of the budgets of various federal agencies to implement U.N. policies. This is a story which must be told if we are to expose the magnitude of this international rip-off and defeat the U.N.'s global tax agenda.

This story has important budgetary and constitutional implications. As long as the true cost of U.N. operations is concealed from the American people, they will be more likely to support continued funding of the world body and may even be tempted to support some form of international tax, on the ground that the cost of the U.N. is just "pennies a day."

Constitutionally, this is an important story because it shows that the U.S. Congress is already being by-passed by federal agencies working in collusion with the U.N. It is time for Congress to hold hearings on this subversion of our form of government.

In my first book, *Global Bondage*, I described this problem in terms of how the U.N. operates as another liberal lobby. I noted that U.N. bodies such as the World Health Organization were part and parcel of Hillary Clinton's campaign to socialize the health care establishment in the U.S. In retrospect, this is not too surprising. It is inevitable that various levels of government, even on an international level, would work together to increase governmental interference in our private lives. This danger would dramatically increase with global taxes.

Federal collusion with the U.N. is critical. One argument against the notion that a U.N. tax could never pass is that Congress would never pass it. This assumes it would be submitted to Congress and not sneaked through the back door, such as through an executive agreement with, say, the G-7 countries. However, it could also be argued that a global tax is already in effect, masquerading as taxes for "domestic" programs.

One example is how the Clinton administration collaborated with the U.N. organizers of the Habitat II U.N. conference in Istanbul, Turkey, in June of 1996. Untold millions of dollars were spent by the U.S. Department of Housing and Urban Development (HUD) to prepare a report in advance of the conference. HUD Secretary Cisneros named a National Prepatory Committee to put it together. The result was a fifty-page report, "Beyond Shelter: Building Communities of Opportunity," issued on 23 May 1996 at a national press briefing on Habitat II arranged by HUD and the U.S. Agency for International Development (AID). The "official" sponsors of this briefing were the World Resources Institute and the Society of Environmental Journalists.

Though ostensibly devoted to the housing issue, the report included such recommendations as "using the educational system as a catalyst for positive social change . . . establishing universal health insurance by the year 2000 . . . [and] financing health insurance through insurance payments combined with general revenue taxes." Obviously, this report served as an excuse to push a variety of liberal initiatives, many of them having nothing to do with housing.

Even more significant, however, was the process that led up to the report:

> As part of the national preparatory process for Habitat II, the U.S. Department of Housing and Urban Development and the U.S. Agency for International Development jointly sponsored a series of 12 town meetings throughout the Nation. . . . Each town meeting was planned and implemented by a local organizing committee with planning support provided by the U.S. Network for Habitat II, a network of nongovernmental organizations dedicated to providing citizens with a voice in the decisions that affect their lives and communities.[1]

An obvious questions is, what role is Congress playing in all of this? Isn't Congress supposed to be the vehicle to provide citizens with a voice? These nongovernmental organizations (NGOs) are critical to understanding how the U.N. by-passes Congress. The process involves the development of networks of liberal Left groups, active on education, housing, and other issues, which will then work to implement, in conjunction with the federal agencies, the recommendations of U.N. conferences. It is a morally and legally objectionable procedure because federal dollars are being used to lobby against the interests of American taxpayers who don't even know what's going on.

In the Habitat II case, one of the members of the HUD National Preparatory Committee was Mencer Donahue Edwards, otherwise known as Don, of the U.S. Network for Habitat II. His group is one which received support from HUD and AID. In his remarks at the 23 May conference, he referred to the groups in his network as "community-based organizations," which are, nevertheless, NGOs at the U.N. On the surface, it may not make much sense for a "community-based" group to have an international connection. However, in terms of implementing an agenda outside of normal democratic channels, it makes perfect sense. The U.N. agenda is being implemented by these groups directly. Edwards himself referred to the NGOs as "the day to day legs" of how treaties and global "plans of action" are enforced. These groups, he said, have "a different version of how this country can be organized." This is an understatement. Their agenda is to completely remake American society.

In a column endorsing global taxes, Jessica Mathews of the Council on Foreign Relations reported that NGOs, which she called "citizens' groups," have a "rapidly growing relationship" with the U.N., which will be "strengthened" by their involvement. How? Through the provision of more revenue. These are the groups which will be creating the appearance of "public support" for global taxes.

But, if Habitat II does not produce a treaty for Senate ratification, then how will the NGOs implement its agenda? The media have left Americans in the dark about these behind-the-scenes activities. As Laurel Heiskell of Concerned Women for America (CWA) explains,

> The U.S. Constitution requires that any foreign treaty be ratified by two-thirds of the Senate. Many treaties produced by the U.N. were never ratified because of their extreme proposals. But in recent years, U.N. conferences have substituted policy statements called "Platforms of Action." They have asked member nations to support these platform documents. Members are then expected to implement these platform documents.
>
> One recent example of this process is the U.N. women's treaty, the Convention on Elimination of All Forms of Discrimination Against Women (CEDAW). Although President Carter signed this radical treaty, it has not yet been ratified by the Senate. More recently, however, President Clinton signed the Beijing Platform for Action, which embodies all the principles of CEDAW. Because Congress is not favorable to the Beijing agenda, the executive branch is circumventing the constitutional process of Senate ratification.[2]

This process of implementing the Beijing document, produced by the U.N.'s 1995 Fourth World Conference on Women, is enlightening. Donna Shalala, secretary of the Department of Health and Human Services (HHS) who served as co-chair of the official U.S. delegation to Beijing, was in charge of this effort, formally titled the President's Interagency Council on Women. This group issued a news release in which Shalala declared, "Our job is to take the agenda of Beijing and, where appropriate, fill in the blanks."

The group included representatives from thirty federal agencies and offices. Hillary Rodham Clinton served as honorary chair of the council.

This news release described the organization as "charged with coordinating the implementation of the Platform of Action adopted at Beijing" and developing "related initiatives to further women's progress and engage in outreach and public education to support the successful implementation of the Conference agreements."

Dr. James Dobson of Focus on the Family was alarmed by the effort, saying "The Platform of Action, which lesbian activists and radical feminists have been lauding, would damage the institution of marriage and undermine the moral principles that support it. It would also promote abortion and safe-sex ideology around the world."[3]

It is difficult to get a handle on how much all of this costs. In the area of U.N. peacekeeping, however, we do have an estimate on how much money has been taken out of federal agencies. A March 1996 General Accounting Office report, entitled "Peace Operations: U.S. Costs in Support of Haiti, Former Yugoslavia, Somalia and Rwanda" found that the administration from 1992 through 1995 provided $6.6 billion for U.N. peacekeeping operations out of the following agencies: Department of Defense, Department of State, Agency for International Development, Department of Agriculture, Department of Justice, Department of

Commerce, Department of the Treasury, Department of Transportation, and Department of Health and Human Services. Yet, the report found that the U.N. had reimbursed the U.S. only $79.4 million for some of these costs.

Of the remainder, $4.8 billion still needs to be reimbursed. No one, of course, believes the U.N. will pay us back, and it's unlikely that the Clinton administration even wanted to be reimbursed. This is because the administration wanted to expand the U.N.'s military activities without going to Congress for additional funding, subverting the will of the legislative branch.

However, Bob Dole was the senator who requested that GAO report. He said that even this figure may be low and that, when other peacekeeping operations are included for the same time period, "the total exceeds $10 billion." He called the funding of U.N. peacekeeping "out of control," adding that it's "illegal" to run other government programs in this manner, long after congressional appropriations have been exhausted.

This controversy gets to the heart of constant claims by the U.N. and the liberal media that the United States has been a "deadbeat" and hasn't paid its "dues" to the world body. The *Washington Post* went so far as to blame the Republican Congress for this, saying the U.S. owed more than $1 billion to the U.N. In fact, the withholding of payments to the U.N. began during the Reagan administration when the House was controlled by Democrats. A bipartisan consensus emerged that the U.N. was not reforming itself and that withholding payments was the only practical way to spark real reform.

Again, however, the claim that the U.S. owes money completely ignores the billions of dollars—perhaps tens of billions—that the Clinton administration has provided to the U.N. out of the budgets of various federal agencies. The possibility that the Congress will not tolerate continued looting of the Department of Defense and other agencies for the U.N. is another reason why global taxes are so desperately needed.

On another front, Tom DeWeese of the American Policy Center charges in his November 1995 "Insider's Report" newsletter that the Convention on Biological Diversity, a treaty that failed to obtain Senate ratification in the 103d Congress, is being illegally implemented. "The Biodiversity treaty literally lays down the plans for a 'reversal' of the process of civilization, ultimately overseeing the herding of people into pre-selected, isolated enclaves, while the rest of America becomes vast wilderness," he points out.

More importantly, he adds, the Global Biodiversity Assessment (GBA), a document mandated by the treaty, is being carried out through Presidential Executive Orders and federal agencies, especially the Department of the Interior. The results are already apparent: predators like wolves and bears are being reintroduced into the Western states; mining and timber companies are facing severe restrictions; property owners are being jailed on wetlands or endangered species violations; and Yellowstone National Park has been granted special "protection" by the U.N.

The Yellowstone case is a very good example of how even a nice-sounding treaty can be manipulated by federal agencies. Acting under the auspices of the

World Heritage Treaty, which was passed in 1972, the Clinton administration's Department of the Interior assumed the costs of bringing a foreign delegation from the World Heritage Committee to Montana from Europe. No congressional approval for this intervention was sought. The delegation made a visit to the park to determine whether the proposed construction of a gold mine a couple of miles outside the park posed some kind of danger.

This may sound fairly innocuous, except for the fact that the U.S. already has a law on the books, the National Environmental Policy Act (NEPA), which covers the matter. Richard Lawson of the National Mining Association quite properly commented in that organization's newsletter that it appeared that the Department of the Interior was trying to set up "an unparalleled separate U.N. review process." Sen. Conrad Burns of Montana was outraged that the U.N. was interfering in U.S. domestic law.

Equally significant, the U.N. delegation started discussing an eighteen-million-acre buffer zone outside the park, affecting ranching, recreational use, timber, oil and gas, and more. It was estimated that forty percent of the "buffer zone" was private property. Here, too, U.N.-affiliated NGOs played a key role. They had signed a letter to the World Heritage Committee in February of 1995 requesting that Yellowstone be put on a list of sites "in danger."

In Australia, which has also ratified the treaty, U.N. interference has generated a significant backlash. Australian businesses and communities have asked that a moratorium be placed on listings under the treaty because sites are being "protected" and "buffer zones" being created without proper consultation, no rights of appeal and a lack of compensation for those who lose their land or resources.

Another example of the executive branch bypassing Congress to further the U.N. agenda is the work of the President's Council on Sustainable Development (PCSD), an initiative of President Clinton designed to fulfill a commitment at the 1992 Earth Summit for "a plan" to confront environmental problems. The PCSD effort, which took three years and reportedly cost $6 million, featured twenty-five leaders from business, government, environmental, civil rights, and Indian organizations. The co-chairs were Jonathan Lash of the World Resources Institute and David T. Buzzelli of the Dow Chemical Company. No identifiable conservatives were named to the panel.

Henry Lamb of the Environmental Conservation Organization called the final report a "blueprint for the reorganization of society" into one that is "centrally planned and managed." He explained, "The recommendations proposed by the PCSD cover the full range of human activities: from building permits to the bedroom (population control); from wilderness to waste; from behavior modification instead of education to a 'managed' economy instead of free enterprise."

How will these recommendations be implemented? At the 23 May 1996 conference preceding the U.N.'s Habitat II conference, Lash announced that the PCSD would continue in operation, and that HUD Secretary Henry Cisneros would become a member. This suggests that HUD may become the lead agency in charge of implementing the policies. However, Secretary of the Interior Bruce Babbit and Environmental Protection Agency administrator Carol Browner were also members, and their agencies could play key roles as well.

Of all the recommendations in the PCSD report, perhaps the most objectionable is the manipulation of young people into service on behalf of the U.N., to help them participate in what are called "global communities." A group called Friends of the Future (FOF) is highlighted as the wave of the future. In Kentucky, the report says, the FOF organization of seventh-, eighth-, and ninth-grade students from St. Francis of Assisi School in Louisville is working to "incorporate environmental and sustainable development education into the Kentucky school curriculum."

The report adds, "Through the sponsorship and support of the U.N. Development Program, FOF published the book, *We Got the Whole World in Our hands: A Youth Interpretation of Agenda 21*, which documents the proceedings of the 1992 U.N. Conference on Environment and Development. The book puts Agenda 21 into simple language—easy for younger readers to understand."

The fact that the U.N. is intervening directly into the U.S. public schools should not be too surprising. This has been going on for decades. In fact, the U.N. connection is quite open, since the U.N. charter mandates that member-states cooperate in educational activities designed to further the aims of the world body. Article 55 of chapter 9 of the charter says that the U.N. shall promote "educational cooperation," and article 56 says that "all member states pledge themselves to take joint and separate action in co-operation with the Organization for the achievement of the purposes set forth in Article 55." This is a convoluted way of saying that the nations which belong to the

U.N. will pursue development of a common educational approach.

For in-depth examinations of our educational problems, I strongly recommend *Outcome-Based Education: The State's Assault on Our Children's Values* by Peg Luksik and Pamela Hobbs Hoffecker (published by Huntington House) and a Research Manual on Goals 2000 compiled and edited by James R. Patrick and published by Citizens for Academic Excellence in Moline, Illinois. Both books highlight the importance of the U.N.-sponsored World Conference on Education for All in 1990.

Regarding the U.N. connection here, the U.S. Office of Education and the Department of State in the late 1940s issued a 108-page report, "The Treatment of International Agencies in School History Textbooks in the United States," which was designed to serve as a basis for changing American history textbooks to favorably highlight international institutions such as the U.N.

This has been quietly proceeding. The Ethics and Public Policy Center released a 1978 report, "How the Cold War is Taught," analyzing six high-school history textbooks. In a section on how these textbooks treat the U.N., the report found that the textbooks gave "undeserved credit" to the U.N., unfairly gave "a boost" to the U.N., and suggested that the U.S. should have relied more heavily on the world body.

Today, at all levels of public education, American students are being conditioned to believe that patriotism is dangerous or naive, and that the solutions to our problems lie in the United Nations and other globalist institutions. The full role of the Department of Education in this campaign is not completely known.

But, it figures to get worse in the years ahead. A federally funded set of national "history standards" for textbooks in the public schools recommended that students examine the case of U.S. State Department employee Alger Hiss, who was not identified as a Soviet spy, in the context of understanding "the emergence of McCarthyism and its impact on civil liberties." The standards did not explain that Hiss was a top aide to President Franklin Roosevelt, was convicted of perjury for denying he was a Soviet spy, and was a key organizer of the United Nations.

Instead, the standards presented the United Nations as a worthwhile "international peacekeeping organization." Students were supposed to examine where it has promoted peace in the world, not whether the U.S. should belong to it or not. Another section advised students to explain the organization and functions of the U.N. using visual aides.

The standards accurately described what the Nazis did to the Jews as "genocide" and suggested that students be exposed to "eyewitness accounts, oral history, testimony of Nazi officials, and documentary photographs and films." But, nothing comparable was suggested so that students could understand the brutality of communism, which killed far more people, and how the U.N. historically served as a front for the Communists and their interests.

The real lesson of history being ignored in these federal standards is that the opponents of communism were right about the danger we faced. They should be given the historical credit they deserve, in the same way that opponents of Hitler and the Nazis are honored for their contributions.

Indeed, these standards contained a glaring omission—a failure to explain the stakes involved in the historic struggle between communism and freedom. The standards said, "The swordplay of the Soviet Union and the United States rightfully claims attention because it led to the Korean War as well as the Berlin airlift, Cuban missile crisis, American interventions in many parts of the world, a huge investment in scientific research, and environmental damage that will take generations to rectify." Notice that the Soviet Union was let off the hook and that "swordplay" was simply blamed. In other words, the United States and the Soviet Union are both morally responsible. And, "environmental damage" was described as a by-product of the victory over Soviet-style communism.

Equally significant, North Korea wasn't held accountable for its invasion of South Korea, and North Vietnam's invasion of South Vietnam was described merely as "involvement" in a neighboring country. Students were told that the American withdrawal from Vietnam was not a failure of will but a demonstration of "the power of American public opinion in reversing foreign policy." The Soviet takeover of Eastern Europe at the end of World War II was explained as a "desire for security" on the part of the Communists.

But, that's not all. It was supposed to be drummed into young people that anticommunism or the "Red Scare" resulted in national "hysteria." The emphasis is not on communism being a real threat to the United States but on those people whose lives were supposedly disrupted by anticommunists such as Sen. Joseph McCarthy. But, revelations out of Soviet archives, as well as the monumental work, *The Secret World of*

American Communism, demonstrate, in the words of former *New York Times* journalist Hilton Kramer, that the congressional investigations of communism in the 1950s "were fully justified." The Communist threat was real indeed.

It's true that some aspects of the history standards are being rewritten because of the outrage which greeted their politically correct outlook. But, pro-U.N. propaganda is already circulating widely through the public educational system.

In fact, the campaign to indoctrinate young people in favor of globalist notions is also apparent in such private organizations as the Boy Scouts of America, now offering a Citizenship in the World merit badge highlighting the U.N. This merit badge is mandatory to attain Scouting's highest rank of Eagle. At the end of the booklet for this merit badge, Scouts are asked questions such as:

> Is the meaning of citizenship changing as the world becomes more interdependent?

> How does the changing world environment affect the responsibilities of United States citizens?

Of course, the implications are that citizenship in the U.S. is an old-fashioned concept in this new "interdependent" and "changing" world. One can imagine students being conditioned in the future to accept the idea of global taxes.

In conjunction with the U.N.'s fiftieth anniversary celebrations in October 1995, a coordinated effort was launched to intensify this kind of approach to education. The U.N. itself offered a "Global Teach-in," in which schools worldwide were "encouraged to dedi-

cate a day or even a week to the study of the United
Nations and the issues on its global agenda."

Toward this end, the U.N. distributed "School
Kits on the United Nations"—curriculum guides—for
all primary, intermediate, and secondary school levels
in all six official U.N. languages. In addition, a
√ "Teacher Training Module on global education and
the U.N. was prepared for primary, intermediate and
secondary school teachers and teacher trainees," designed for use with the school kits. It is not clear how
widely these are in use.

One U.N. brochure stated:

> While the diplomatic community and academia
> will focus on the fundamental global issues,
> educators are hoping to use the anniversary to
> stress the need for international cooperation to
> the young generation—from elementary school
> students to college graduates. Educational
> projects are a staple of all national programs,
> with Ministries of Education and Teachers
> Associations in many Member States enthusi-
> astically joining the "Global teach-in" project
> developed by the UN 50 Secretariat. The an-
> niversary will also give a major boost to Model
> UN programs, a classroom exercise simulating
> the work of various UN bodies, which are being
> held in an ever growing number of countries.
> High on popularity lists are essay and photo
> competitions, poster and poetry contests and
> debating sessions.

Other suggestions in connection with the Global
Teach-in were to "declare an official Global day, week,
or month for the Teach-in through your district, organization or school" and to "organize Teacher Train-

ing workshops for introducing global issues and the UN into lesson plans."

The target audience even included children ages three and four. Special episodes of the childrens' program "Sesame Street" were being planned for the week of 24 October, U.N. Week, "to reach the preschool audience" with pro-U.N. messages.

One particularly insidious document, *A World in Our Hands*, received wide distribution. Published "In Honor of the 50th Anniversary of the United Nations" and featuring a foreword by U.N. Secretary General Boutros Boutros-Ghali, it was said to be "written, illustrated and edited by young people of the world." In fact, the young people turn out to be between the ages of twelve and twenty-one! The book endorsed a World Supreme Court, a Global Peace Force, a U.N. Youth Service, and even U.N. TV. The book was put together by a group called Peace Child International, a group that sponsors "international youth exchanges."

In addition to the U.N. itself, the pro-U.N. educational lobby in the U.S. includes the United Nations Association of the U.S. (UNA-USA), which maintains a "campus network" that involves student leaders on five hundred campuses in pro-U.N. activities. UNA-USA is the group which stages Model U.N. programs involving sixty thousand high-school and college students.

Another component is the Academic Council on the United Nations System, an international association of "scholars, teachers and others" who share a "professional interest in encouraging and supporting education and research which deepen and broaden our understanding of international cooperation." The council works closely with the U.N. and the United Nations University.

Still another is the National Council for the Social Studies, which produced the document, *Citizenship in the Twenty-first Century*, covering such topics as "Citizenship in a Global Environment." It also produces buttons and bumper stickers advising students to "become a global citizen."

Finally, there is the National Education Association, well-known promoter of globalist education and Goals 2000 Outcome-Based Education, all of which emphasize student participation in the "global economy."

Endnotes

1. "Beyond Shelter: Building Communities of Opportunity," The United States Report for Habitat II, U.S. Department of Housing and Urban Development, May 1996, 43.

2. "Implementation in the U.S.," *Family Voice*, vol. 18, no. 5 (May 1996): 7.

3. Dr. James Dobson, Dear Friend letter, January 1996, 4.

Global Reconstruction

3

The death in May 1996 of Chief of Naval Operations Admiral Jeremy "Mike" Boorda, one of the navy's most respected and accomplished officers, was attributed to concerns that he was about to be accused of wearing war medals he didn't deserve. It was said that he killed himself because he feared being disgraced. Others said it was because of political correctness infecting the navy and influence from feminists.

Several weeks earlier, however, in a speech at a Naval Institute conference, former Navy Secretary James Webb had referred to other pressures on the U.S. military. Webb said these were "uniquely difficult times for military leaders" because of several factors, including the fact that "new concepts of limited war" were being imposed from above on the Department of Defense. This was an unmistakable reference to increased U.S. involvement in no-win U.N. military operations at the expense of maintaining a superior national defense.

The navy—the nation's historic first line of defense—had been hit especially hard by the "downsizing" of the Clinton era. The number of air-

craft carriers was reduced from sixteen to twelve, and
nuclear-powered carriers were all but eliminated.

As early as 1994, the administration's budget was
not providing enough to maintain U.S. readiness levels, as evidenced by reports that three of the army's
twelve divisions were not combat ready. The General
Accounting Office in July of 1994 reported a $150
billion gap between what the administration said it
wanted the military to do and the funding levels it
provided for the military.

It would have been one thing if the reductions
had been accompanied by the withdrawal of U.S. troops
from abroad, perhaps for redeployment to America's
porous southern border, and the diminution of the
foreign threat. However, the fall in defense spending
was occurring despite the rise of Islamic fundamental-
ism, the emergence of China, the reemergence of Iraq,
and Russia's increasingly threatening and nationalistic
course. Rather than address these concerns, the Clinton
administration was cutting defense while building up
the military forces of the U.N. and getting U.S. forces
involved in U.N. missions all around the globe. This
had the effect of diverting resources from the basic
military mission of national defense.

The results were quite extraordinary: In 1996, according to the Department of Defense, the U.S. itself
had 72,000 troops deployed in support of U.N. operations, costing untold tens of billions of dollars. The
U.N. had about 70,000 other troops directly under its
own control in sixteen different countries of the world,
bringing the grand total to almost 150,000 worldwide. The U.N. had arrived as a global military super-
power.

Even though the Clinton administration was looting the budgets of the Pentagon and other federal agencies to the tune of $6.6 billion to help pay for some of these U.N. military operations, the U.N. still owed over $1 billion to countries supplying troops to the effort. The problem was that the U.N. was getting involved in so many operations around the world so fast—without having the resources to pay for them—that the countries supplying the troops were themselves not getting paid by the U.N. From the perspective of the U.N. and its supporters, there is only one answer: global taxes.

Financial management has never been a strong suit at the U.N., and the ideological fervor of some pro-U.N. groups supersedes mundane considerations about where the money is going to come from. However, there are some organizations with a traditional antidefense bent which are actively involved in the campaign for global taxes, recognizing that the U.N. needs billions of additional dollars in order to really be an effective military force. These groups have come to the realization that the U.N. can't keep spending money it doesn't have.

Though considered to be antidefense here in the U.S., it is apparent that some of these organizations are not opposed to military activities around the world but are mainly concerned about under whose auspices they are conducted. For these groups, the U.S. military mission is objectionable, but the U.N. is supposed to have loftier motives. In the words of the U.N. charter, the world body protects "peace and security." Some organizations on the far Left of the American political spectrum actually believe this to be true.

One of the members of the advisory council of the Global Commission to Fund the United Nations is Admiral Gene LaRoque (retired), chairman of the Center for Defense Information (CDI), an organization considered to be on the far Left of the political spectrum. The commission is one of the leading organizations promoting global taxes.

Col. Daniel Smith (retired), the CDI associate director, authored an article for the journal *Futures* advocating more international revenues for U.N. peacekeeping activities. However, the proposal he reviewed involved setting up a United Nations Security Insurance Agency (UNSIA). Under the scheme, the U.N. would authorize UNSIA as a "public/private partnership corporation" that would sell insurance to weaker and poorer countries for less than it would cost them to operate and maintain a military establishment. If a country belonging to UNSIA was threatened, it could call on the U.N. to intervene with peacekeeping forces. Smith reported:

> In support of the UNSIA concept, The Center for Defense Information has begun an initial canvass of existing risk assessment tools and models used by international agencies, government departments, multinational corporations, think tanks, insurance companies, and higher-level US military colleges.[1]

Still another proponent of global taxes for military purposes is the World Federalist Association, a group promoting "world federation"—a euphemism for world government—which claims ten thousand members in the U.S. Its president is John B. Anderson, a former Republican congressman who ran for president in 1980 as an independent. Alluding to the U.N.'s military role, the group has urged its members to oppose any effort by the Republican Congress to cut funding for the U.N., adding,

> Looking toward the future, we must find additional, independent sources of financing. Taxes on arms sales, while a good "sin" tax, do mean the U.N. becomes partially dependent upon the revenue generated by these sales. More viable sources of income may be taxes on international air travel or postal service, taxes on international financial transactions—all these activities benefit from the maintenance of international peace and security which the U.N. is expected to provide.[2]

Though regarded by some as just a fringe organization, the World Federalist Association awarded its Global Governance Award in 1993 to Strobe Talbott, who served as deputy secretary of state in the Clinton administration. Talbott, as a columnist for *Time* magazine, wrote an article declaring that "it has taken the events in our own wondrous and terrible century to clinch the case for world government."[3] Perhaps global taxes are designed to bring this about.

An international organization called the Independent Commission on Population and Quality of Life also proposed a new source of global revenue for U.N. peacekeeping operations. However, this organization suggested that SDRs (Special Drawing Rights)—a special form of international currency—be used

> in order to instill an element of automaticity and allow for a speedy deployment of peacekeeping operations, the United Nations should be allowed recourse and access to Special Drawing Rights (SDR). To this end the Articles of

Agreement of the International Monetary Fund
(IMF) would need to be revised so as to permit
the allocation of SDRs in another way than
currently envisaged, restricted to peace-related
activities.[4]

In my first book, *Global Bondage, The U.N. Plan to
Rule the World*, I explain how the U.N. Charter establishes a system whereby the nations of the world disarm by providing armed forces and other assistance to
the U.N. The plan is outlined in Chapter VII of the
U.N. Charter.

Oscar Arias, the former president of Costa Rica,
is pushing a variation of such a "global demilitariza-
tion" plan which includes an "international code of
conduct" for the sale of weapons, to be presented to
the U.N. He wants developing nations to abandon
their armies, much as Costa Rica did, in return for aid
from multilateral institutions such as the World Bank.
In fact, he wants these international agencies to tie
their lending to promises and commitments from these
nations to disarm.

A proposal was considered during the Kennedy
administration to establish a U.N. "Peace force" that
would replace the arms of the nation states. It was
spelled out in a State Department document entitled
"Freedom from War: The United States Program for
General and Complete Disarmament." This plan urged
the "disbanding of all national armed forces and the
prohibition of their reestablishment in any form what-
soever other than those required to preserve internal
order and for contributions to a United Nations Peace
Force."

In 1960, Paul Nitze, who became JFK's assistant
secretary of defense for International Security Affairs,

proposed at a seminar in California "a series of unilateral actions" to slow down the arms race, including putting the U.S. Strategic Air Command under a "NATO Command" and then telling the U.N. "that NATO will turn over ultimate power of decision on the use of these weapons to the General Assembly of the United Nations."

The Clinton administration carried a variation of this plan forward in a big way. Following Boutros-Ghali's call for activation of article 43 of the U.N. charter and the establishment of a permanent U.N. army, President Clinton issued Presidential Decision Directive 25 (PDD 25), beginning a formal process of integrating U.S. and U.N. military forces. Despite some protests from Republicans, the administration put U.S. forces in U.N. military operations in Somalia, Macedonia, and Haiti. In Bosnia, to avoid criticism, Clinton technically put U.S. troops under the command of NATO, although the Implementation Force (IFOR) which was deployed there became a regional organization under the U.N. charter.

In Bosnia, Clinton appeared to be following the advice of those, like international financier George Soros, who believe that NATO should play the role of preeminent world body until the U.N. acquires more power and competence.

In a 1993 speech, "Toward a New World Order: The Future of NATO," Soros declared,

> The United Nations might have become an effective organization if it were under the leadership of two superpowers cooperating with each other. As it is, the United Nations has already failed as an institution which could be put in charge of U.S. troops. This leaves NATO

as the only institution of collective security that has not failed, because it has not been tried. NATO has the potential of serving as the basis of a new world order in that part of the world which is most in need of order and stability. But it can do so only if its mission is redefined. There is an urgent need for some profound new thinking with regard to NATO.

Soros, who met regularly with Clinton and Deputy Secretary of State Strobe Talbott, seemed to be describing precisely what is happening to NATO in Europe and Bosnia today. The Bosnia peace agreement explicitly made NATO an arm of the U.N. in article 6, which describes how the Implementation Force (IFOR) of NATO and non-NATO troops will operate. The agreement explicitly says that the U.N. Security Council is "invited to authorize Member States or regional organizations and arrangements to establish the IFOR acting under Chapter VII of the United Nations Charter." This means that IFOR becomes a U.N. operation, fulfilling the New World Order vision of Soros.

The "new thinking" Soros talked about was also reflected in Clinton's decision to install a Spanish Socialist as the head of NATO. Although Clinton has emphasized that the overall military commander in Bosnia is an American general, George Joulwan, the fact is that Joulwan responds to NATO political control, and NATO's political control is represented by the North Atlantic Council and its head, Secretary General Javier Solana.

The Bosnia deployment could be described as a "limited war" or no-win operation, conducted under the auspices of the U.N. These were having a major impact on the U.S. Army, whose leadership was also under heavy pressure to toe the line.

Former foreign service officer Harold Eberle, now with the South Carolina Policy Council, has made the convincing case that the Bosnia deployment is illegal and unconstitutional because the troops have been used for offensive purposes, thus violating the North Atlantic Treaty, and are deployed in a country that is not a signatory to the treaty.

But, this is just the start of what Soros and others have in mind. In an April 1995 article entitled "Ambushing the Future," which appeared in the Special Warfare publication of the U.S. Army JFK Special Warfare Center, the special forces were put forward as what one U.S. Army soldier, Sfc. Edward B. Rasor, described as the "reconstruction tool for the New World Order." Rasor, based at Ft. Bragg, found the article so offensive that he began openly questioning the direction of the army and its involvement with the U.N. For this, Rasor's military career was scheduled for early termination by army headquarters and the White House.

The article, written by James J. Schneider, a professor of military theory at the School of Advanced Military Studies at the U.S. Army Command and General Staff College in Fort Leavenworth, Kansas, included the following:

> The future will be dominated by a resurgent force that will change the nature of both the nation-state and the national security system. . . .

> We have yet to divine the full implications of the revolution in geopolitics euphemistically called the new world order.

For the Army, and for Special forces, the future will be a period of global reconstruction.

But, there is another aspect of reconstruction that anticipates the future—the army's unique relationship to the U.S. Constitution.

As an army we are fortunate to have such a rich historical tradition. But, this experience is of little use if it cannot be interpreted in light of future operations. In other words, to learn from the past we must anticipate the future. And, the future will be dominated by a single overwhelming presence—the United Nations.

One of the key legal strands was the right of the state to declare and wage war. The growing power of the U.N. is beginning slowly to erode this defining characteristic of the nation-state. Now, the U.N. has begun to redefine victory on its own terms.

The U.N. redefinition of victory has also set the stage for redefining the purpose of a nation's armed forces. The reemergence of the United Nations has created a new formula: Under the new U.N. arrangement of collective security, nations will strive primarily to compel peace. The U.N.'s central role in shaping the future during global reconstruction will persist, and its geopolitical influence will likely increase.

What the article leaves unanswered, of course, is who will pay for this kind of "global reconstruction." If the past is any guide, the U.S. taxpayers will pick up most of the bill. However, opposition is likely to come not only from taxpayers resisting the imposition of global taxes but American soldiers themselves and—hopefully—some military leaders.

Sergeant Rasor, of course, was not the first to object to participating in "global reconstruction" on behalf of the U.N. The first was U.S. Army Specialist Michael G. New, who was court-martialed, convicted of disobeying a lawful order, and given a bad conduct discharge for resisting deployment to a United Nations military operation run by a Finnish general in the former Yugoslav republic of Macedonia.

Saying, "I signed up for the green team, not the blue team," New told his superior, "Sir, I took an oath to the Constitution of the United States of America. I cannot find any reference to the United Nations in my oath or in the Constitution I have sworn to defend." His oath committed him to obeying orders if they are consistent with the U.S. Constitution, military regulations, and the Uniform Code of Military Justice.

The oath says, "I will solemnly swear (or affirm) that I will support and defend the Constitution of the United States against all enemies, foreign and domestic; that I will bear true faith and allegiance to the same; and that I will obey the orders of the President of the United States and the orders of the officers appointed over me, according to regulations and the Uniform Code of Military Justice, so help me God."

As New's parents put it, "Michael New did not take an oath to defend the United Nations or its charter. Instead, he took an oath which he understood to be exclusive to the United States of America." As part of the deployment, New was required to alter his army uniform with United Nations patches and wear a U.N. blue beret or helmet. He was also required to carry a U.N. identity card, confirming his transformation into a U.N. soldier without American POW/MIA protections.

The American people supported New in over-whelming numbers. Literally thousands of letters were sent to Michael by well-wishers, and dozens of members of Congress wrote to President Clinton asking for "a full legal and constitutional analysis of the justification of your orders placing members of the United States Armed Forces under the 'command' of foreign United Nations officers." Legislation was introduced in both Houses of Congress to prohibit the president from forcing our troops to wear any of the U.N. symbols that constitute the U.N. uniform.

At a news conference announcing support for this legislation in the House, Rep. Tom DeLay, the House Majority Whip, declared, "A soldier's oath is to the U.S. Constitution, not to the UN Charter. Forcing soldiers to wear the uniform of the United Nations effectively asks the soldier to serve another power. No American soldier should be put in Michael New's position—forced to choose allegiances between the United States and the United Nations." DeLay said about New, "He is willing to fight and die for his country, but he is not willing to fight and die for the United Nations. Frankly, I can't blame him."

In the other body of Congress, similar legislation was introduced by Sen. Larry Craig with the support of Senate Majority Leader and GOP presidential candidate Bob Dole. However, Dole, who said he would fight any Democratic attempt to "force U.S. soldiers to fight and die under U.N. command and in U.N. uniform," refused to speak out specifically on New's behalf. Sen. Phil Gramm, another GOP presidential candidate who declared opposition to U.N. command of our troops and cosponsored the Craig bill, also failed to support New specifically.

Patrick J. Buchanan, who emerged as leading Republican contender with Dole for the presidential nomination, at first balked at supporting New, calling it a case of obeying the "legitimate orders of his commander." Buchanan said that New "should not disobey orders and as one who aspires to be commander-in chief, I don't think you can tell an American soldier to disobey orders."[5] However, after carefully researching the case, Buchanan changed his position, declaring unequivocal support for New and hailing his courage and bravery. Support for New became a common theme in his presidential campaign speeches, and he vowed, as president, to pardon Michael New, saying "where were Bob Dole and Phil Gramm when Michael New needed them?"

Although the judge in the case ruled that it was a lawful order before giving the case to the military panel, evidence produced in the court-martial proceedings conclusively demonstrated that the president did not have the right to order our troops to wear U.N. uniforms or make them report to foreign commanders. New's defense team convincingly demonstrated that there is no basis in law or the Constitution for President Clinton's pro-U.N. policy.

New's lead attorney, Col. Ron Ray (retired), noted that New got into trouble initially for asking a basic question, By what authority do I wear a United Nations uniform? Ray pointed out that New was not necessarily against the U.N. In fact, he had served in a U.N. operation called Southern Watch in Kuwait. The difference then was that New participated in a U.S. uniform and reported to an American commander. This is why when he was told that he was being assigned to Macedonia and would wear a U.N.

uniform and report to a U.N. commander, he asked his blockbuster question, By what authority?

Ray said the question was never answered because the policy has not been implemented in accordance with the Constitution and Defense Department and Army regulations. "The reason they didn't answer it is that there is no authority," he said. The army eventually conceded that the U.N. uniform was not authorized.

Ray called the treatment of New an indication of how "compromised" the army has become—"the degree to which our military is willing to accommodate political pressures which do not stand constitutional or legal scrutiny."

Could similar pressures have had anything to do with Admiral Boorda's death?

For his part, Michael New took the honorable course. Speaking at an April 1996 conference sponsored by the American Sovereignty Action Project, his father, Daniel New, said, "Don't feel sorry for Michael New. He gets to stand up with the likes of Patrick Henry, the likes of Nathan Hale, the likes of George Washington and say, 'I love my country.'"

He said Michael was taught love for country and love for God and had become "a bright light in a dark place." For that, he was extremely thankful. "I have never been more inspired by any person in American history than my own son," he said.

Following New's example, more soldiers are coming forward to resist the pro-U.N. agenda. However, they are not seeking to undermine military morale, order, and discipline. Instead, they stand as evidence of the breakdown in these areas that already exists as a result of the pro-U.N. policy. The American people must understand that we are losing many good soldiers on this particular altar of political correctness.

New and Rasor are only the most visible manifestations of the problem. Col. Robert Maginnis (retired) of the Family Research Council, though critical of New's position, himself said he believed that many soldiers are troubled by the military's growing involvement in U.N. peacekeeping. "With thousands of U.S. forces wearing the U.N. uniform," he told the *Washington Times*, "it goes through the mind of every soldier, airman and sailor: Who is it I am representing?"

Washington Times journalist Rowan Scarborough quoted an Army medic at Fort Bragg as saying about New's stand, "I think that it is very widespread, and I think it's an opinion that is almost universal among all soldiers."[6]

Moreover, the U.S. Army itself has substantial evidence that American soldiers are showing increasing "resistance" toward U.S. involvement in "peacekeeping" missions. In fact, the U.S. Army is so concerned that its Research Institute for the Behavioral and Social Sciences has underwritten research to analyze the attitudes of U.S. Army soldiers to involvement in such operations.

One study, conducted by David R. Segal of the University of Maryland, found that members of two U.S. Army units, the Fourth Battalion, 505th Parachute Infantry Regiment (4-505-PIR), and the 10th Mountain Division, were extremely resistant to involvement in "peacekeeping" operations. In 4-505-PIR, Segal found that "a plurality of the soldiers were noncommittal on whether peacekeeping was appropriate for their unit, and while over a third agree that it was appropriate, one out of five soldiers disagreed. In the

10th Mountain Division, rejection was even more extreme. A majority of the soldiers felt that peace-keeping missions were not appropriate for their unit."[7]

Navy Lt. Comdr. Ernest G. Cunningham, who wrote a thesis on the subject, noted that when soldiers fail to believe in such a mission or "in their governing authority's competence to make these decisions, unit cohesion suffers."[8]

Cunningham's thesis, "Peacekeeping and U.N. Operational Control: A Study of Their Effect on Unit Cohesion," included asking a group of marines if they would swear to the following code: "I am a United Nations fighting person. I serve in the forces which maintain world peace and every nation's way of life. I am prepared to give my life in their defense." The answer: 69 percent refused. The survey also found that 73 percent opposed U.N. control of our troops and 67 percent did not believe the president has the authority to pass his responsibility as commander in chief to the U.N. secretary general.[9]

Finally, the marines were asked for their response to this one:

> The U.S. government declares a ban on the possession, sale, transportation, and transfer of all non-sporting firearms. A thirty (30) day amnesty period is permitted for these firearms to be turned over to the local authorities. At the end of this period, a number of citizen groups refuse to turn over their firearms. Consider the following statement: I would fire upon U.S. citizens who refuse or resist confiscation of firearms banned by the U.S. government.

On that key question—firing on Americans resisting confiscation of their firearms—one out of four indicated yes. However, those who answered negatively on the firearms question were adamant, using what were described as "heavier pen or pencil marks on their response or written comments in the margin" of the survey. The comments included "Hell No!" and "If you take our [Constitutional] Amendments away, then you can take this job and stick it where the sun don't shine."

Perhaps another survey could ask the question whether U.S. soldiers serving the U.N. would fire on Americans resisting collection of their global taxes for purposes of "global reconstruction."

The emergence of a military-oriented publication called *The Resister* suggests the answer may be no. This organ, representing the views of military personnel who choose to remain anonymous, openly advocates anti-U.N. resistance.

But, the U.N. and its supporters want global taxes not only for expanded U.N. peacekeeping operations but for the creation of international structures to carry out and enforce what they believe will be global disarmament leading to world peace.

Former antiwar protester President Clinton apparently agrees with them. He declared a unilateral ban on nuclear testing but resisted deployment of a missile defense for the United States. A missile defense would greatly lessen the pressure to negotiate a "deal" on nuclear weapons through the U.N., and would restore America's ability to act independently in world affairs.

Clinton, putting his faith in the U.N., was insisting on a "total ban" on nuclear tests. One obvious problem is that Russia can't be trusted to comply. Another is that both China and India, the two most populous nations on earth, have refused. China, meanwhile, is supplying India's archrival Pakistan and Iran with nuclear and missile technology, and India is threatening to deploy nuclear weapons unless a test ban treaty includes a timetable for "total and universal disarmament," presumably under U.N. auspices. This would entail teams of U.N. inspectors running around the world supposedly making sure that countries disarm.

However, the notion that the U.N. could monitor and enforce "total and universal disarmament" is laughable in light of Iraq's well-documented ability to fool the U.N. Iraq was a signatory to the Nuclear Non-Proliferation Treaty, a document negotiated under U.N. auspices that was supposed to prevent the development of nuclear weapons.

Herbert Krosney, who writes about the arming of Iran and Iraq in his explosive book, *Deadly Business*, told me, "It is striking how many different weapons systems the Iraqis were going after. They went after the 'Supergun,' a long-range cannon, two or three different ways to get the atomic bomb, a poison gas program, and a biological weapons program. They were going after everything in an extremely ambitious way." And, they were assisted by France, Britain, Germany, and the United States.

The Persian Gulf War, waged under U.N. mandates which prevented total victory over Iraq, apparently resulted in the destruction of this program. However, it's impossible to know for sure. The U.N. set up a commission to determine the full extent of the Iraqi program and to make sure Iraq doesn't rearm. However, this commission has been repeatedly forced to review what it thinks it knows about the

Iraqi program, and *U.S News & World Report* reported that the U.N. commission itself included suspected agents of Iraq.

One of the latest revelations by the head of the commission, Rolf Ekeus, was that the Iraqis even tried to develop "radiological weapons," which scatter radioactive material. These are neutron bombs, non-explosive nuclear devices.

Dr. Sam Cohen, the developer of America's now-defunct neutron bomb program, tells me these low-yield nuclear devices can never be effectively outlawed because they are already in production in countries such as Russia and can be made small enough to be dropped by a terrorist into a trash can across the street from the White House.

Those who put their faith in the U.N. also have yet to explain how they will disarm Iran, whose nuclear program is supported by both China and Russia. Iran could have a nuclear bomb in as early as five years, and Krosney says the Iranian problem could be far more serious than Iraq because the Iranian rulers are motivated by fundamentalist Islamic ideology. "It's a far more dangerous situation," he told me. "You have the potential of a bomb being used by terrorist elements or by the Iranian regime itself."

A critical question, he says, is whether Israel would decide to bomb the nuclear reactors in Iran that may produce the nuclear bomb-related materials. Today, Krosney argues, Israel is not prepared to stage a military strike like the one it conducted in 1981 on the French-supplied Osirak nuclear reactor in Iraq. A strike on Iran, he warns, "could lead to a major war" in the Middle East. Krosney believes one factor behind Israel's desire for a comprehensive Middle East peace is fear of an Iranian bomb.

Such a "peace" could come about under U.N. auspices, enforced by U.S. and Russian peacekeepers. The U.S. and Russia have been staging joint "peacekeeping" exercises for several years now.

Another troublesome country is Libya, which is developing a major chemical weapons program. The U.N. solution, once again, is a treaty, the Chemical Weapons Convention negotiated under the auspices of the U.N. This treaty, which is supposed to ban chemical weapons, passed the Senate in April of 1997. However, a spokesman for the committee, chaired by Sen. Jesse Helms, who voted against the treaty, said it had been told by the U.S. intelligence community that compliance with the document could not be verified. Kathleen Bailey, who works for Lawrence Livermore National Laboratory, says a chemical weapons plant could be small enough to be hidden in a commercial warehouse. "There are no technical means to locate secret chemical installations," she points out.

Nevertheless, under pressure from the Clinton administration, the Joint Chiefs of Staff in March of 1996 deleted an $805 million defense budget item to modernize American chemical warfare defenses. Journalist James Ring Adams called this decision, which was quickly reversed, "dangerous." It came in the wake of the revelation by one of Clinton's own panels, the Presidential Advisory Committee on Gulf War Veterans' Illnesses, that U.S. equipment to detect chemical agents during the Persian Gulf War was inadequate and unreliable.

The Department of Defense and Iraq both claim that the Iraqis did not use chemical or biological agents during the war. Some experts believe that the thousands of veterans suffering from Gulf War Syndrome were the victims of the drugs they were given to guard against a chemical weapons attack. Others think exotic diseases are playing a part. However, U.S. troops could have been exposed to low levels of chemical agents over a period of days or even weeks, producing cumulative toxic effects.

In a February 1995 article in *The American Legion Magazine*, I first reported evidence that the Russians had developed a new kind of chemical weapon and had it tested on our troops by the Iraqis in the Gulf War. Dr. Michael Waller of the American Foreign Policy Council told me that he was told by Russian scientists, including Vil Mirzayanov, that the weapon—called Novichok—also affects human genes, causing birth defects and infant illnesses among offspring.

In a 30 April 1996 article in the *Wall Street Journal* entitled "Russia's Toxic Threat," James Ring Adams confirmed all of this, quoting Mirzayanov, who has since fled to the West, as warning that U.S. soldiers during the Gulf War "may already have been exposed to minute quantities of this nerve gas without knowing it." Mirzayanov "says that an agent called Substance 33 may have been in the hands of Iraq during the Gulf War and that the accidental or other discharge of small quantities, undetectable by American instruments, could have produced some of the symptoms called Gulf War Syndrome," Adams reported.

But, the push for U.N.-sponsored "disarmament" is hard to resist, even for military leaders who want to appear fashionable. The Clinton administration in 1996 largely succumbed to another U.N. campaign, this one to ban defensive laser weapons. William Taylor, a combat veteran and senior vice president for

International Security Affairs at the Center for Strategic Studies, pointed out that the purpose of these weapons was "to save lives—the lives of American and allied servicemen and women," and called the effort to ban them "multilateralism threatening the basic, sovereign interests of the United States of America."

Another U.N. campaign, to "ban" land mines, was also largely successful. President Clinton in May of 1996 endorsed a permanent worldwide "ban" on their use even while allowing our own military to temporarily use them in confrontation areas like the Korean demilitarized zone. The U.S. Army had viewed land mines as an important defensive weapon, with Joint Chiefs Chairman General John Shalikashvilli calling them "indispensable" during the Gulf War. But, the U.N. campaign against them was supported by former military leaders such as Gen. Norman Schwarzkopf and Gen. David Jones.

The logical outcome of this campaign to have the U.N. supervise the "disarmament" of the world in all of these different areas is that sensitive U.S. intelligence information is being handed over to the world body, ostensibly for the purpose of monitoring compliance with international agreements and facilitating peacekeeping operations. This was done increasingly in the Clinton administration. Indeed, Clinton claimed the unilateral authority to transfer this information to the U.N., and his person in charge of assisting the U.N. in this regard was Assistant Secretary of State for Intelligence Tobi Gati, a former vice-president of the pro-U.N. lobbying group, the U.N. Association. Gati told the House Intelligence Committee in 1995 that there had been "very few" unauthorized disclosures of U.S. intelligence information provided to the U.N.

However, former Assistant Secretary of Defense Frank Gaffney noted that, in one episode, U.S. intelligence which had been shared with the U.N. and marked NOFORN (not to be supplied to foreign nationals) was nearly left behind when the U.N. abandoned Somalia. This unsecured cache of sensitive U.S. intelligence materials had been discovered by American forces covering the withdrawal of U.N. forces from the country.

Gaffney questioned the intelligence sharing arrangement with the U.N., noting that the organization is "largely staffed with civil servants detailed from foreign intelligence services." Historically, the U.N. has been a hotbed of Communist espionage operations. For a time, the U.N. undersecretary general in charge of peacekeeping was an Iraqi, Ismat Kattani.

Henry Hyde, a member of the House Intelligence Committee, points out that secret intelligence should be the nation's early warning system. In the Revolutionary War, he notes, our forefathers limited knowledge of key secrets to only five people, each of whom took an oath of secrecy. One of these secrets was France's covert support of the revolution.

But, how things have changed.

At the CIA in the Clinton administration, Enid C. B. Schoettle served on the National Intelligence Council (NIC) as the National Intelligence Officer for Global and Multilateral Issues. Prior to joining the NIC, where she served as a key adviser to the director of Central Intelligence, she was a senior fellow and director of the Project on International Organizations at the Council on Foreign Relations (CFR).

She is also one of the authors of the CFR work, *An Agenda for Funds: The United States and the Financing of the United Nations*, which was being advertised as recommending ways "to ensure that the UN has the financial resources to fulfill its expanding role in the world."[10]

Her position seems to be that the U.S. has a duty to share intelligence with the U.N., and that American taxpayers have an obligation to pay for it. All of this is being done in the name of unverifiable and unenforceable U.N.-sponsored global disarmament agreements which will leave America vulnerable.

Endnotes

1. Daniel M. Smith, "The United Nations Security Insurance Agency (UNSIA) Proposal," *Futures*, vol. 27, no. 2 (March 1995): 211.

2. "U.N. Funding" leaflet, Campaign for Global Change, World Federalist Association, 1995.

3. Strobe Talbott, "America Abroad," *Time*, 20 July 1992.

4. Dragoljub Najman and Hans d'Orville, *Towards a New Multilateralism: Funding Global Priorities. Innovative Financing Mechanisms for Internationally Agreed Programmes* (New York: Independent Commission on Population and Quality of Life, 1995), 5.

5. Buchanan appearance on CNN's "Evans & Novak," 7 October 1995.

6. Rowan Scarborough, "Most troops said to oppose U.N. role," *Washington Times*, 24 November 1995, 1.

7. David R. Segal, "Constabulary Attitudes of National Guard and Regular Soldiers in the U.S. Army," 11.

8. Ernest G. Cunningham, "Peacekeeping and U.N. Operational Control: A Study of their Effect on Unit Cohesion," (Master's thesis, Naval Postgraduate School, 1995), 19.

9. Ibid.

10. "Forthcoming Titles," *Council on Foreign Relations* (Spring/ Summer 1995): 1.

Life Unworthy of Life

As the United Nations assumes the trappings of a world government, it is becoming increasingly clear that nice-sounding phrases like "women's rights," "sustainable development," and "family planning" are being used by the world body to sanction authoritarian control over the most intimate details of our private lives. As I put it in my book, *Global Bondage*, "The clear intention of the birth control effort from the beginning was not to give individuals the right to make decisions, in the privacy of their own bedrooms, but rather to 'empower' government to regulate and control the human species for its own purposes. This is a philosophy that works to the benefit of totalitarian regimes, be they Communist, Nazi, or Fascist."

Another nice-sounding phrase that is appearing more frequently in this campaign is "quality of life." In fact, a group called the Independent Commission on Population and Quality of Life has emerged to argue for more effective means to control population growth and therefore ensure a "quality of life" for those who survive. Its members include Eleanor Holmes Norton, the congressional representative for the District of Columbia in the U.S. Congress, and

Juan Somavia, the main organizer of the 1995 U.N. World Summit for Social Development, where global taxes were discussed and promoted.

This group produced a May 1995 document entitled *Towards a New Multilateralism: Funding Global Priorities. Innovative Financing Mechanisms for Internationally Agreed Programmes.* The document, a virtual catalogue of global tax proposals, was written by Hans d'Orville, a German national who served as an assistant secretary of the UNDP, and Dragoljub Najman, a Yugoslav national who served as assistant-director general of UNESCO (The U.N. Educational, Scientific and Cultural Organization).

The Independent Commission on Population and Quality of Life is supported, by its own account, by the governments of Canada, Germany, Japan, the Netherlands, Norway, Sweden, and the United Kingdom, the U.N. Population Fund, the World Bank, the Ford Foundation, the William and Flora Hewlett Foundation, the MacArthur Foundation, the Andrew W. Mellon Foundation, the Rockefeller Foundation, the International Planned Parenthood Federation, and the Population Council.[1] These are powerful forces in the forefront of the movement for global taxes.

It's important to understand the U.N. perspective on population. Because it takes a resolute stand in favor of open borders, it has nothing but contempt for U.S. efforts to prevent the illegal entry of three to four million Mexicans a year into the U.S. The world body will say that it opposes "trafficking" in people for monetary purposes, but will not oppose the movement of individuals by themselves across borders. In fact, the U.N. objected when California passed Proposition 187, cutting off welfare for illegal immigrants.

In terms of population, the U.N. wants every nation to be like the U.N.—multicultural in make-up and outlook. This spells the demise of nation-states. It may already be too late to prevent America from undergoing an unprecedented transformation that is threatening our heritage and survival.

America's immediate threat is a movement of Mexicans—here and abroad—who are actively plotting to get the territory taken during the Mexican-American War, which they call Aztlan, returned to Mexico. Their aim is to take it back by re-occupying our southern states. As part of this, Mexican President Ernesto Zedillo has proposed an amendment to the Mexican Constitution allowing Mexicans to retain their nationality when they take out American citizenship. Zedillo said to them, "You're Mexicans—Mexicans who live north of the border."

So, the influx of illegals is not an "accident," caused necessarily by bad economic conditions. It is a deliberate policy, in the same way that communism was a frontal attack on the American way of life.

The refrain that "America is a nation of immigrants" is true. But, current immigrants from Mexico are different. They don't want to learn English and don't want to be Americanized. An American citizenship ceremony in Arizona in 1994 was conducted largely in Spanish and, in a case to be decided by the U.S. Supreme Court, an Hispanic state government employee in Arizona fought for the "right" to conduct state business in Spanish. Through the federal government, as part of complying with the Voting Rights Act, we as taxpayers are actually forced to provide them with bilingual ballots so they can take political power through the ballot box without ever learning English.

The answer to this problem, of course, is to enforce our laws and protect our borders. The U.N. would have us believe that the answer lies in government-mandated population control programs around the world, in Mexico, and everywhere else.

The U.N. Conference on Women, which was held in Communist China in 1995, demonstrates how insidious and dangerous this international campaign has become and how, with global taxes behind it, it could result in the quick emergence of a global population control program that could make Nazi Germany look tame by comparison.

Leaving aside the problem that the conference was held in a country, Communist China, where a woman's "reproductive rights" are controlled by the state, the entire agenda of the event was designed to undermine the natural differences between the sexes, discredit the traditional family, and obliterate the notion of motherhood. Why? Because the U.N.'s notion of "family planning" translates into not just population control but depopulation. Traditional families mean lots of children. The world body aims to limit and reduce the number of people by isolating, attacking, and manipulating mothers who have the potential of giving birth to children. For the U.N., mothers are the enemy because they produce children.

In pushing this agenda, the U.N. hopes to play on common fears about growing numbers of people, especially in the Third World. On the face of it, the numbers do seem striking: there are 5.7 billion people in the world, and China alone has 1.2 billion, almost five times as many people as the U.S.

But, rather than restrict population growth and control people's lives, the U.N. and the U.S. government would be better advised to support policies that promote economic growth and development. This is one way to make sure that people don't flee their own countries for a better place, which usually turns out to be America. In Mexico, however, there is a Socialist regime heavily in hock to the International Monetary Fund (IMF).

The way out of the population "crisis" is giving people the freedom and responsibility to care for themselves, their families, and their nations. But, that eliminates the influence of U.N.-affiliated institutions such as the World Bank and the IMF in the internal affairs of member-states.

The "option" of more freedom and opportunity runs directly against the agenda of those who want more government control, including a world government, that will dictate family life. The U.N. planners contend that people destroy the environment, rather than contribute to it. Therefore, they must be controlled, even eliminated. Individual freedom and responsibility, within a context of traditional values, do not fit into their "Brave New World." And, big families are certainly an obstacle to their plans.

The U.N. Population Fund, one of the largest U.N. agencies, implements this population control program in more than one hundred countries. National Institute of Womanhood President Cecilia Acevedo Royals describes how it works: "Mothers in Kenya must stand by helplessly while their children die of simple pneumonia because their clinics, chocked full of costly IUD's, do not have a single vial of penicillin that costs only a few cents; women in India are lured into government sterilization chambers with promises of houses and loans; women in many developing communities must submit to taking contraceptives before their community gets a new road, or a waterpurification tool."

The use of economic and financial blackmail to reduce population will undoubtedly intensify. The Clinton administration's Undersecretary of State for Global Affairs Timothy Wirth met with the president of the World Bank, James D. Wolfensohn, who indicated that the bank is prepared to provide the financial means to implement the Beijing conference agenda. Wolfensohn is described in his official biography as having "a long record of involvement in development and environment issues" and served on the board of the Population Council, a private group pushing the U.N. population control strategy.

If threats don't work, there's always pure force. The scheduling of this "women's conference" in China, though controversial, was no accident. It is relevant to what the U.N. planners ultimately have in mind for those women around the world who want to have children and families. In China, a woman can be forced to have abortions or undergo sterilization to comply with the state-mandated one-child-per-family policy. If a mother somehow manages to have more than one child, government benefits can be taken away or her children killed outright.

In China, because of the custom of male heirs, this has meant the disproportionate slaughter of females. A glimpse into this "Brave New World" was provided in 1995 when some American news magazines carried stories and photos of how children in Communist Chinese orphanages are routinely and deliberately starved to death. The orphanages were said to have higher death rates than even some of the

Nazi death camps. One picture showed an emaciated eleven-year-old girl tied down to a bed, withering away to nothing. A British documentary on the problem, *The Dying Rooms*, showed children tied to wooden toilets, sleeping in their own excrement. Another emaciated child was filmed on a table wasting away with a serious eye infection that had gone untreated. One of the British reporters was shocked when a towel on a cart started moving and crying; a baby was hidden underneath it, left alone to die.

But, the key point—often overlooked in the stories about the orphanages—is that this is being done with the assistance of the United Nations. The U.N. Population Fund has poured an estimated $150 million into the Chinese population control program over the years. The killing of these babies is a direct result of the Chinese one-child-per-family policy, implemented with the assistance of the U.N.

Newsweek was honest enough to point out, "The vast majority of kids in Chinese orphanages are not orphans at all, but abandoned children. They're almost always girls, victims of the government's one-child-per-family policy and the traditional peasant preference for boys." This is the policy being supported by the U.N. in China.

In the British film, academic Stephen Mosher pointed out that the policy, instituted back in 1979, was implemented after Western experts from the World Bank and the United Nations told China that they had to control their population for economic reasons. Explaining some other ramifications of the one-child-per-family policy, he said some babies are born and immediately drowned or have a lethal injection shot into their bodies through the soft spots on their skulls.

Sen. Jesse Helms, chairman of the Senate Foreign Relations Committee, has set the record straight about the U.N.'s involvement with the Chinese program: "For almost two decades, UNFPA [the U.N. Population Fund] has, in the name of reducing the world's population, helped the Communist Chinese Government manage its brutal population control program. Under China's program, women are dragged into government clinics and forced to have an abortion if they already have one child. Women and men are forced, like animals, to undergo sterilization procedures if they violate or oppose the 'one-child' policy. This inhumane program—which UNFPA upholds as a model for developing countries—has caused an alarming increase in abortions of baby girls because many Chinese consider them less valuable."

Helms noted that UNFPA's current executive director, Ms. Nafis Sadik, told China's official news agency in 1991 that "China has every reason to feel proud of and pleased with its remarkable achievements made in its family planning policy and control of its population growth over the past 10 years. Now the country could offer its experiences and special experts to other countries."

However, the Chinese program is still evolving. In June of 1995 a law went into effect in China mandating automatic abortions for fetuses judged to be "defective" (i.e., retarded or having spina bifida). Can the murder of the elderly be far behind? As many as eighty million people were killed in China as part of the Communist revolution. A few million more wouldn't make any difference to the Communist dictators.

Though publicized by our own media, the story about the conditions in the Chinese orphanages actually demonstrates how bad a job our media have done in covering Communist China. When our nation's top journalists were in China reporting on that so-called women's conference sponsored by the United Nations, they completely missed this story. It appears that either they were not interested or were taken on guided tours of Chinese orphanages where the babies appeared to be well treated.

The sad fact is that many in our media, especially female journalists, want to ignore the Nazi-like nature of the Chinese program because of the perception that women in China are making progress in other areas, such as the economy and politics. In connection with the women's conference, for example, CNN anchor Judy Woodruff wrote a long article for the *Washington Post* that devoted only one line to the issue of mandatory abortions for women having more than one child. Bonnie Erbe, host of the public television program "To the Contrary," went so far as to favorably quote Chinese Communist mass killer Mao Tse Tung as saying that "women hold up half the sky." Erbe hailed the Communist Chinese constitution for supposedly guaranteeing "equal rights" for women.

American journalists in China may be reluctant to expose human rights abuses because they fear they will be evicted from the country. In December 1995, for example, the Chinese Communist regime announced the expulsion of a leading German journalist. He was charged with writing articles that "attacked personalities of the People's Republic" and of having "negatively influenced German public opinion about China." In fact, he had only written about human rights problems and corruption in China.

The U.N. complicity in the killing of baby girls in China makes a complete mockery of what the U.N. says it represents. The shocking fact is that, in the name of protecting human rights, the U.N. actually works to destroy them. However, the U.N. planners rationalize this by insisting that population control is absolutely necessary to save the earth and protect it from human beings.

How can a global organization encouraging baby-killing be sincerely interested in protecting the rights of girls or boys? The obvious answer is that the U.N.'s drive for "children's rights" is a sham designed to put more power and authority into the hands of international bureaucrats. With global taxes at their disposal, the U.N. could dramatically expand its population control program.

Not surprisingly, however, the U.N. still doesn't want to fess up to its complicity in the Communist Chinese brand of "family planning." A current U.N. document, "The Girl Child," calling for a "global agenda for girls" around the world, promotes the U.N. Convention on the Rights of the Child, another dangerous treaty authorizing government interference in family affairs. In the hands of the U.N., it could actually be twisted into sanctioning the outright murder of children.

In this area, like many others the U.N. injects itself into, the organization desperately needs more money to expand. A first step was taken when the Clinton administration restored taxpayer funding for the U.N. Population Fund, which financially supports Communist China's one-child-per-family policy. The

U.S. now provides the U.N. agency with $55 million a year.

In addition, under the Clinton administration a policy decision was made to regard women who flee China and resist forced abortion and forced sterilization as criminals who should be deported back to China. Under previous administrations, such women were considered candidates for asylum in the U.S.

Rep. Christopher Smith's (R-N.J.) House Subcommittee on International Operations and Human Rights had a hearing on this issue in 1995, featuring Chinese women who had been forced to undergo abortions under the regime's one-child-per-family policy. One of those victims told Smith, "If we don't have the right even to give birth to a baby, what's the use of any other rights?"

But, the Clinton administration recognizes the "human right" to abortion, not the human rights of unborn children.

Although we might like to think so, it is not likely that the United States will ultimately be spared from a Chinese-style population control program. Here, for the time being, so-called family planning is being pushed with tax dollars mostly on poor people and teen-agers. Eventually, however, it will likely lead to government-imposed restrictions on the size of families.

There is already a proposal on the table, introduced by Lester Brown of the Worldwatch Institute, to discourage population growth in the United States by changing the tax structure. Currently, American families can take deductions from their taxes for as many children as they have. But, Brown says, "The time may have come to limit tax deductions for children to two per couple. It may not make sense to subsidize childbearing when the most important need facing humanity is to stabilize population."

For the time being, the strategy in the U.S. stops just short of outright coercion and changing the tax code. However, the cost of raising children has risen dramatically because the personal exemptions for children have not kept pace with the cost of living.

Current plans, directed at girls and young women, call for more efforts at educational brainwashing, the establishment of more school-based "health clinics" and school-based "health information programs" and more "family planning" efforts in local communities.

Cecilia Royals of the National Institute for Womanhood says the U.N. is attempting to move the U.S. and other governments toward a situation in which a young woman will be "educated" for the purpose "of ensuring that she seeks greater use of contraception, abortion and sterilization and selects any occupation, other than motherhood." The document prepared for the Beijing women's conference explicitly attacked "traditional female and males roles that deny women opportunities for full and equal partnership in society" and called for the development of "curricular and teaching materials" to break down these roles.

At the same time, the U.S. Congress is continuing to fund scores of "family planning" projects throughout the U.S. that attempt to manipulate a woman's "reproductive rights" and control the size of families. This money—$193 million in fiscal year 1995—is funneled through Title X of the Public Health Service Act and goes to many Planned Parenthood affiliates that promote and perform abortions.

Despite talk of a "revolution" when the Republicans took control of Congress in 1994, the Republican-controlled House voted 221 to 207 to continue this program, demonstrating there is really not a dime's worth of difference between the two parties on an issue dear to the hearts of big government liberals.

Much of this money is provided to buy condoms and other contraceptives for teen-agers. This may sound reasonable in light of the skyrocketing illegitimate birth rate. But, the facts show that it has been a colossal failure, perhaps deliberately so.

As noted by Gracie Hsu of the Family Research Council, "even though more teenagers are being exposed to these family planning 'services,' the rates of out-of-wedlock births, abortions, sexually-transmitted diseases, and pregnancies have all risen significantly in the teenage population since the [Title X] program's inception." She says the program has failed largely because it by-passes parental rights and authority. Without such guidance and without a foundation of strong moral and religious values, teen-agers who are provided with sexuality information and even contraceptives are more likely to engage in sexual activity and have children, abortions, or get sexual diseases.

So, why does this failed program continue? One answer is that a multibillion dollar birth control industry dispensing chemicals and pills to our young people has a vested interest in continuing it. Another is that the failures serve as an excuse for government to take even more intrusive action into our private lives to "control" the problem that government has made worse! This is why the U.N. is involved on a global basis. The issue can be manipulated into giving the world body even more power to run our lives.

With global taxes, the Chinese program could be expanded on a worldwide basis.

In the U.S., the population control movement is so strong that it came perilously close to capturing the post of surgeon general. Dr. Henry Foster, President Clinton's nominee to replace the embarrassing Dr. Joycelyn Elders as surgeon general, was closely associated with Planned Parenthood. He had performed an unknown number of abortions, had supervised a study using drugs to induce abortions, and had endorsed fetal experimentation and human embryo research. He had also engaged in the involuntary sterilization of the retarded—a practice reminiscent of Nazi Germany.

Despite this hideous record, Foster actually had a majority of votes in the Republican-controlled Senate to win the post. However, he failed to get the sixty votes necessary to derail a filibuster staged by Sen. Phil Gramm, and his nomination died. Were it not for Gramm, the U.S. might have gotten an abortionist as surgeon general—a person who is supposed to defend life would instead have been a destroyer of it. America seems to be closer to the "Brave New World" of the U.N. planners than many of us are prepared to admit.

It wasn't until recently that we were aware of the horror of "partial birth" abortion, a procedure in which a baby is partially delivered, its brains sucked out and head crushed, and then disposed of. Brenda Pratt Shafer, a registered nurse who witnessed the procedure, testified, "The baby's little fingers were clasping and unclasping and his feet were kicking. Then the doctor stuck the scissors through the back of the head and the baby's arms jerked out in a flinch. . . . The doctor opened up the scissors, stuck a high-powered suction tube into the opening and sucked the baby's brains out. Now the baby was completely limp."

The practice of euthanasia continues to attract a lot of attention in the U.S. because of the activities of Dr. Jack Kevorkian, accused repeatedly of murder by helping people kill themselves. Euthanasia has been defined in almost benevolent terms as inducing a pain-less death in elderly people who are sick or dying. But, once euthanasia is accepted for some people, under what seem like ethical circumstances, it can be ex-pected that the practice will be applied by government to others against their will. In this regard, Nazi Ger-many serves as a concrete example of how a govern-ment-run euthanasia program works in practice.

The book by Michael Burleigh, *Death and Deliv-erance: Euthanasia in Germany*, chronicles the Nazi attempt to eliminate its "unfit" members. The book demonstrates that between 1939 and 1945 the Nazis systematically murdered as many as two hundred thou-sand mentally ill or handicapped people who were said to be "life unworthy of life." All of these murders were completely legal and considered ethical at the time.

Of course, this program was just a small part of the Nazi "race purification" campaign that eventually took the lives of six million Jews.

While Hitler engineered this onslaught, he per-sonally disapproved of the killing of animals and was a vegetarian. This is not dissimilar from the prevailing mindset in America, where the lives of human be-ings—especially the unborn, the elderly, and the handi-capped—are increasingly in jeopardy, and the lives of "endangered" animals are protected by federal law and federal agents.

It is not inconceivable that America could soon witness the widespread "mercy killing" of the elderly and the handicapped—anyone, in the words of the Nazi planners, who is considered "life unworthy of life."

Nevertheless, because these practices are clothed in the rhetoric of compassion or because they are viewed as an effort to grapple with the population "problem," they are likely to be accepted by growing numbers of people. This opens the door for global taxes to finance a drastic expansion of these programs on a worldwide basis.

In order to stop this onslaught, we have to expose the myth of family planning, that the issue isn't what people do in their private lives but the role of government in regulating or controlling these decisions for us. Those who are pushing population control aim to use government to force us to conform to their agenda. The deadly secret is that family planning is a cover for government control of our families and our lives!

On an international level, the Roman Catholic church is battling against this U.N. "vision" for humanity. According to Vatican insider Malachi Martin, author of *The Keys of This Blood*, Pope John Paul II believes there will be world government by the year 2000,[2] but opposes the U.N. agenda for the world because he believes the U.N. is proabortion and prohomosexuality and wants to destroy the traditional family.[3]

In this connection, there is continuing controversy over the attempted assassination of the pope. Some experts believe the Communists were behind the assassination attempt on Pope John Paul II because of his ultimately successful effort, working with the

Reagan administration, to destabilize the Communist puppet government in his native Poland. But, Martin suggests that the real culprits lie beyond communism—secular and humanist forces opposed to the Catholic church position on contraception, abortion, and the need for Christ-centered education.

In his "Gospel of Life," in an unmistakable reference to the U.N. and other global players, the pope condemned the "powerful of the earth" and the "international institutions" engaged in what he called a "conspiracy against life" and designed to bring into being a "culture of death."

Catholic writer Suzanne Rini, author of *Beyond Abortion*, says we are witnessing the emergence of an "antiChristian social order" whose "religion" is eugenics, the scientific improvement of the human race by deciding who will live and who will die, based on their "quality of life."[4] Ultimately, she writes, the objective is "a scientized Garden of Eden," in which human beings will literally be designed and "created" by others. Under one possible scenario, a genetically based "utopia" will be achieved "and the Fall and sinful nature of man repudiated."[5]

Rini specifically points to the dangers inherent in the "Human Genome Project," an "effort to map and sequence the entire human genome," the approximately one hundred thousand genes in the human body.[6] This project could produce the research necessary to produce a master race. The program, budgeted at $3 billion and coordinated by the National Institutes of Health, is supposed to have located the one hundred thousand or so human genes and completely analyzed the structure of DNA by the year 2005. Though presented as an effort to identify hereditary illnesses, some fear the project will inevitably lead to the automatic, even required, abortion of genetically "imperfect" offspring.

But, Rini says it could go in another direction, the creation of what could be seen as subhumans. Human embryos could be created in the lab and defined under the law as chattel or property, she says. "Corporations, then, could try to genetically engineer humans to create a compliant work force," she explains.

This effort is always referred to as "multinational" in scope, in the sense that many different nations are pooling their resources in order to complete the project. Currently, programs are also underway in Britain, France, the European Community, and Japan. But, the word *multinational* could also imply a United Nations connection down the road, perhaps through the World Health Organization.

Commenting on the possibilities, writer Monette Vaquin said:

> Today, astounding paradox, the generation following Nazism is giving the world the tools of eugenics beyond the wildest Hitlerian dreams. It is as if the unthinkable of the generation of the fathers haunted the discoveries of the sons. Scientists of tomorrow will have a power that exceeds all the powers known to mankind: that of manipulating the genome. Who can say for sure that it will be used only for the avoidance of hereditary illnesses?[7]

Can humans be trusted with this power as it relates to other human beings? In a column about the controversy over the teaching of creation and evolution in the public schools, Council on Foreign Relations fellow Jessica Mathews put the issue in clear and concise terms for all Americans: "It is about whether human life was created for a purpose or is the result of a random, unsupervised, natural process."

If life is just a random, unsupervised, natural process, then earthly survival is the only goal and humans should be entrusted with the power to decide who lives and dies, based on their value to the species. For those who see life on this earth as the sum and total of all human existence, then it makes sense to eliminate the genetically deficient.

It also makes sense, from this perspective, to harvest body organs from the unborn as well as the living, even if they are prisoners scheduled for execution and consent for the operations is not received. This is also happening widely in China, which has tried to keep it secret. Reports indicate that foreigners make up most of these "customers," willing to pay top dollar for quick access to organs and wanting to avoid long waiting lists for transplant operations here. The transplants are said to be an excellent source of foreign currency.

Endnotes

1. Dragoljub Najman and Hans d' Orville, Towards a New Multilateralism: Funding Global Priorities (Independent Commission on Population and Quality of Life, May 1995), 67.

2. Malachi Martin, interview with author, broadcast over Newstalk Radio Network, 1 August 1994.

3. Ibid.

4. Suzanne Rini, "Open Season on Humanity," *Celebrate Life* (November/December 1995): 32.

5. Suzanne Rini, *Communique*, American Life League, 6 October 1995.

6. See *Justice and the Human Genome Project*, edited by Timothy F. Murphy and Marc A. Lappe (Berkeley: University of California Press, 1994), vii.

7. Ibid., 14.

Back to Nature 5

The arrest in 1996 of the alleged Unabomber terrorist demonstrated the logical outcome of radical environmentalism. Theodore Kaczynski had close ties to radical environmentalist groups and had attended an Earth First meeting at the University of Montana where a "hit list" of "enemies" of the environment was distributed. Two on the list were killed by bombs believed to have been sent by him. His alleged victims included Gilbert P. Murray, the head of a Sacramento, California, timber lobbying group, and Thomas J. Mosser, a public relations executive whose company had done some work for the Exxon oil company.

The philosophy articulated by Kaczynski in his "manifesto" was described as "anti-industrial." This was certainly true. But, as the bombings show, it was also antihuman. It is strange to think of some humans waging war on others for environmental purposes. But, that is the philosophy that Kaczynski apparently embraced. It is a war on people. In fact, John Davis, editor of the *Earth First Journal*, was once quoted as saying that "eradicating small pox was wrong." Smallpox, he said, "played an important part in balancing ecosystems."

Davis is talking about "biodiversity," a term which has a positive connotation in America today and is featured regularly in United Nations literature, usually in connection with the concept of "sustainable development." It is generally considered an attempt to protect plants, animals, and things. But, as Davis's comments on smallpox suggest, it actually has a much more sinister application.

From the point of view of the radical environmentalists, it is a doctrine which holds that every species has equal intrinsic value and that the planet earth cannot be viewed solely as a resource for human beings. In other words, we are the enemy. There are too many of us humans. We pollute the planet. We use too many resources. This may explain why predators such as bears and wolves are being reintroduced into the Western part of the U.S.

When a group of environmentalist organizations in 1995 was agitating for U.N. control over Yellowstone National Park, it sent a letter to a U.N. committee that said the park was "in danger" in part because of "human-bear conflict [which] jeopardizes the grizzly bear." In other words, the bear was important, not the human. The same letter complained about "ever-increasing levels of visitation" to the park by humans and "home building and new population clusters" near the park.

If the bears don't get us, perhaps the environmentalists will. One is Ric Valois, founder of the Environmental Rangers, a radical green group. "A gun enthusiast and military buff, he wears a 9mm sidearm on his hip as he prowls the Blackfoot River near Lincoln, Montana, in search of environmental offenders," a *Washington Times* article said. The *Times* dubbed his group the "green militia" and said that it has threatened violence against miners, loggers, and others.

There is, of course, an important difference between Kaczynski and Valois and the elites who run the environmental movement. Kaczynski was a true believer in the sense that he lived like a virtual caveman, isolated in a cabin and rarely showering. Valois, too, lives in a cabin. But, the CEOs who manage the professional environmental movement make hundreds of thousands of dollars a year and live the high life. They are not so much interested in a "back-to-nature" existence as they are in making sure that the living standards of other people get cut, that we get back to nature, by force if necessary.

In a report by the Center for the Defense of Free Enterprise, entitled "Getting Rich," the financial facts about the wealth and power of the environmental movement are laid out. They are astounding. For example, John Sawhill, president of the Nature Conservancy, pulled down a $185,000 salary; Jay Hair of the National Wildlife Federation got $242,060; and Fred Krupp of the Environmental Defense Fund received $193,558 a year.

The revenue of these organizations was equally impressive. The Nature Conservancy pulled in $278,497,634; the National Wildlife Federation received $82,818,324; and the Environmental Defense Fund collected $17,393,230.

If we don't get shot by the environmentalists, our living standards will certainly continue to suffer. Maurice Strong, the secretary general of the Earth Summit and former director of the U.N. Environment Program, has declared, "It is clear that current lifestyles and consumption patterns of the affluent middle class—involving high meat intake, consumption of large amounts of frozen and convenience foods, use of fossil fuels, appliances, home and work-place air conditioning, and suburban housing—are not sustainable."

The U.N.'s Habitat II conference in Turkey in 1996 gave us another indication of what the U.N. has in store for us and how they intend to accomplish this radical transformation of our lives. As Laurel MacLeod of Concerned Women for America put it, the conference called for the complete "re-design" of cities' regulations, political systems, and judicial and legislative procedures.

One of the greatest enemies, from the U.N. perspective, is the car—a symbol of personal freedom to most Americans. The car is a villain because it pollutes and uses too much energy. In the U.S., Vice President Gore, author of *Earth in the Balance*, wasn't alone in viewing the internal combustion engine as a dire threat. President Clinton disclosed that he once told China's president Jiang Zemin that the "greatest threat" China posed to the U.S. was environmental because the Chinese drive too many cars.

New York Times columnist Thomas L. Friedman said he was told by Clinton that he told the Chinese Communist leader,

> The greatest threat to our security that you present is that all of your people will want to get rich in exactly the same way we got rich. And unless we try to triple the automobile mileage and to reduce greenhouse gas emissions, if you all get rich in that way we won't be breathing very well. There are just so many

more of you than there are of us, and if you
behave exactly the same way we do, you will do
irrevocable damage to the global environment.

Former Secretary of State Henry Kissinger was
even alarmed by this statement, calling it an example
of how Clinton and the "protest generation" had found
America guilty of various "sins" which have allegedly
contributed to the world's ills. Kissinger said Clinton
naively seemed to think that the Communists in China
would respond to this expressed desire for cooperation
on "social issues" when there are so many other areas,
military and strategic, which divide us.

Nevertheless, this single-minded fixation with perceived global threats—and the notion that the whole
world will come together to grapple with them—drives
the environmentalists today.

As long as China refuses to cooperate, citizens in
other countries will be the targets. In an official Habitat II document on the "urban environment," Quezon
City in the Philippines was given credit for staging
"impromptu road inspections" of cars, checking them
for pollution emissions.

The report, put together by the World Resources
Institute, the U.N. Environment Program, the U.N.
Development Program, and the World Bank, also
advocated a wide variety of taxes on the cost of operating a car. The report explained:

> Some countries have begun to consider taxa-
> tion as a means to reduce vehicle use, conserve
> energy, and reduce carbon dioxide emissions.
> Hungary, for instance, introduced an environ-
> mental tax on fuel in 1992 as well as a road
> maintenance fee.

> Fuel taxes can be an important policy tool in
> efforts to change travel behaviors. . . . The high
> cost of fuel in Japan and Europe has led people
> in those countries to drive less and to drive
> more fuel efficient cars than their counterparts
> in the United States.[1]

Here, the city of Chattanooga, Tennessee, is considered a model for the U.N. in "changing behaviors." A Housing and Urban Development Report prepared for Habitat II called it an "environmental city" and a "sustainable community." Residents certainly deserve to be proud of its transformation from the "worst polluted city" in the U.S. in 1969 to the point where in 1990 it was said to have met federal clean air requirements. However, the transformation does not seem to be complete.

Speaking at a conference on Habitat II, City Councilman David Crockett described how city managers have tried to "disconnect" people from their automobiles and "connect them to each other" through more funding of public transportation and the creation of more walking and bike paths. He discussed how city residents have been exposed to a "wholistic" approach to life through "massive education." Apparently, this has come about at least partly through the efforts of the local newspaper, the *Chattanooga Times*, whose publisher, Paul Neely, introduced Crockett to the conference. Neely said the effort in Chattanooga was assisted by grants provided by foundations, whose resources are "based on that old industrial money."

The effort to change behaviors and discourage the use of cars was at least partly behind the Clinton administration's 4.3 cents-a-gallon rise in the gas tax. But, when gas prices started rising in the summer of

1996, congressional Republicans looking for a campaign issue saw their chance to repeal it. In some ways this was a trivial issue. However, higher taxes are rarely justified, and the American people rightly revolted at the high cost of gas. "We can't have everything—cheap energy, ample supply, a safe environment and no intrusive regulation," declared Council on Foreign Relations fellow Jessica Mathews in a *Washington Post* column. But, of course, we can, if we have the political will.

The Mathews column was noteworthy for the failure to recommend more exploitation of our domestic oil resources in Alaska and off the coasts. Mathews complained about rising oil imports, but the policy pursued by her and her friends in the environmental movement force us to rely more heavily on foreign sources of supply.

At the same time, the environmental movement has a burning desire to increase the power of international agencies such as the U.N. This tendency, however, proceeds not on the basis of bombing people into submission but through scare campaigns that provoke more and more government regulation of industry and higher and higher taxes, all in the name of "saving the planet."

It is very costly to finance this dramatic expansion of governmental power, especially on an international level. This is why some of the leading cheerleaders for global taxes are in the international environmental community.

The "need" for these taxes is obvious: the 1994–1995 "World Resources" report of the World Resources Institute (WRI) alluded to the cost of implementing the global environmental agenda at $600 billion. WRI has long been a proponent of "Green Fees," another word for taxes.

Today, it is desperately working to "design effective taxing mechanisms" and is studying ways to "adjust the tax bases" in industrialized countries to favor environmental causes. These are all euphemisms for higher taxes. It is also in favor of implementing a carbon tax in all the countries belonging to the Organization for Economic Cooperation and Development (OECD).

Along these same lines, WRI is examining what it calls "new financial schemes," the "rethinking [of] old institutions," referring to the Global Environmental Facility and the World Bank, and is examining "the availability of new funds under, for example, the Climate Change Convention." This is the U.N. treaty that is supposed to curb global warming.

One immediate threat is the proposed ratification of the U.N. Convention on the Law of the Sea, described by the Clinton administration as "the strongest and most comprehensive environmental treaty in existence or likely to emerge for quite some time." The administration claims some changes have been made in it since the time when President Reagan refused to sign the document in 1982. But, it still includes a new U.N. institution—the International Seabed Authority—to be based on "assessed contributions." The International Seabed Authority is ruled by a "council" which raises revenue from mining. These are dangerous precedents for U.N. global tax schemes.

The nature of this arrangement was recognized by former U.N. officials Erskine Childers and Brian Urquhart, who, in proposing a "United Nations surcharge" on international trade and raw materials or commodities, noted that "there will, of course, be the future revenue from the Seabed Authority," as if this were, indeed, a precedent for such schemes.

The United Nations Association (UNA), the premier pro-U.N. lobbying group in the U.S., recognized the precedent-setting nature of the Seabed Authority as well, noting that "only the Seabed Authority created by the U.N. Convention on the Law of the Sea, which entered into force in late 1994, has authority today to directly collect international revenues to finance its activities."[2]

James Gustave "Gus" Speth, who served as President Clinton's administrator of the U.N. Development Program, is an environmentalist who strongly supports global taxes. He founded the WRI in 1982 and served as its president until January 1993. Before founding WRI, he coordinated President Jimmy Carter's environmental program and helped found the Natural Resources Defense Council.[3]

In the fall of 1994, in advance of the March 1995 U.N.-sponsored World Summit for Social Development, Speth, as UNDP administrator, openly endorsed global taxes. One of his proposals was for "an international tax on the consumption of non-renewable energy" and "global environmental permits" for industries to operate. Speth said, "These proposals demand a great deal from the international community. But they are all doable."[4]

The 1994 *Human Development Report*, issued by Speth's UNDP, was explicit in this regard, calling for "new sources of international funding that do not rely entirely on the fluctuating political will of the rich nations." The report said that some of these proposals include "tradable permits for global pollution" and "a global tax on non-renewable energy."[5]

The 1994 *Human Development Report* went further, adding specifics about the proposed international taxes on energy. It urged "fees" on "polluting emissions" and "a global tax on energy." It said that a tax of $1 on each barrel of oil (and its equivalent on coal) during 1995 through 2000 would yield around $66 billion a year.[6]

At about the same time that the U.N. World Summit for Social Development was being held, the Global Commission to Fund the United Nations was issuing its own report. Entitled *The United Nations at Fifty: Policy and Financing Alternatives*, it was published in the March 1995 issue of *Futures: The Journal of Forecasting, Planning and Policy*. A summary of the proposals said the global taxes could be used "for the tasks which nation states cannot perform successfully by themselves," including grappling with "global environmental issues" and "sustainable human development." It proposed levies on fishing in deep oceans and "sin" taxes on "dangerous" environmental activities.

The Commission on Global Governance also emphasized global taxes for environmental purposes. It suggested "charges on the use of global resources such as flight-lanes, sea lanes, and ocean fishing areas."[7]

In its report, *Our Global Neighborhood*, the group said that "the time could be right" for a "fresh look and a breakthrough in this area." It declared, "The idea of safeguarding and managing the global commons—particularly those related to the physical environment—is now widely accepted; this cannot happen with a drip-feed approach to financing."[8]

The Ford Foundation's 1994 study, "Renewing the United Nations System," by former U.N. officials

Childers and Urquhart, suggested several "schemes for additional financing of the UN." These included global taxes on "the production of materials such as petroleum and hydro-carbons [and] mineral raw commodities."[9] Another group, the Worldwatch Institute, in its 1993 *Report on Progress Toward a Sustainable Society,* called for global taxes to "solidify U.N. finances."[10]

One of the contributors to that 1993 volume, Hilary French, wrote a separate July 1995 report, *Partnership for the Planet: An Environmental Agenda for the United Nations,* which urged development of a "dedicated funding mechanism to finance the investments required for the transition to a sustainable society—including environmental programs." She seemed to prefer an international currency tax in order to generate more money for environmental programs.[11]

The environmentalists perceive they need billions or trillions of additional dollars because their plans are so extraordinarily ambitious. It is not an understatement to say that they want to completely remake human society and alter the American way of life, with the United Nations playing a key role.

To some extent, Americans are waking up to the fact that something strange is going on. Many have noticed the unusual markings on signs entering our state and national parks that refer to them as "biosphere reserves" or "world heritage sites."

Rev. Joseph Chambers of Charlotte, North Carolina, obtained some striking photographs of the sign leading to Mount Mitchell State Park in North Carolina before and after citizens started asking questions about it. One photo of the sign identified the park as a "United Nations Biosphere Reserve." After some

questions were asked about the significance of the
U.N. marking, the sign was changed to read merely
"*International* Biosphere Reserve" (emphasis added).
Part of the sign was simply turned around so the name
United Nations was no longer visible in the front. But,
the words *United Nations* were still visible on back,
until a plank was put over them too.

Park officials vehemently deny that the U.N. in
any way is trying to take over our parks. They changed
the sign just to prevent these wild "conspiracy theo-
ries" from developing. But, if everything is so innocent, why not explain the U.N. role and let the American people make up their own minds about what's
going on?

Suspicions were aroused by that visit in November
of 1995 by a foreign U.N. delegation to Yellowstone
National Park, to agitate against the construction of a
gold mine a couple of miles outside the park. This
visit was arranged and paid for by the Clinton administration. Yellowstone is both a U.N. biosphere reserve and a world heritage site, designated that way
under the terms of a 1972 U.N.-sponsored treaty on
protecting the heritage of the world.

Subsequently, Clinton administration Vice President Al Gore traveled down to the Florida Everglades,
where he announced a $1.5 billion program, paid for
by a tax on sugar production, to return one hundred
thousand agricultural areas—some of the richest farm-
land in America—to marshland. As many as forty
thousand jobs were immediately put in jeopardy.

When Gore announced this plan, he didn't travel
under the U.N. flag, like they did in Yellowstone.
But, the result was still the same. The Everglades is
both a U.N. biosphere reserve and a world heritage

site. Al Gore knew exactly what he was doing; he was a leading participant in the 1992 U.N.-sponsored Earth Summit.

There are currently forty-seven U.N. biosphere reserves and twenty world heritage sites in the U.S. which are being used to create and expand vast wilderness areas and restrict human and economic activity. In fact, experts say that what is being planned is the creation of "Bioregions" and the relocation of human beings, all for the purpose of promoting "sustainable development" or protecting "biological diversity," or "biodiversity."

In the U.S. Northwest, the plan is already well underway. President Clinton's so-called compromise on the Spotted Owl problem was a sell-out to the professional environmentalists which will ultimately result in the loss of eighty-five thousand timber and related jobs. Mr. Clinton's "conversion" plan will, at best, throw a few of the unemployed into make-work jobs. The rest will go on welfare.

Incredibly, one commentator said that, now that Mr. Clinton had the forest problem behind him, he could concentrate on the economy. This is typical of the lack of understanding of how environmentalism costs jobs and hurts the economy. The president's plan will hurt timber production, increase the cost of lumber, and make it harder for new couples to qualify for the purchase of first-time homes. This *will* affect the economy as a whole.

The well-financed green lobby came out the winner, and industry and labor came out the losers. But, in defeat, America may have seen the possibility of a comeback and ultimate victory. In a major development, representatives of industry and labor came together at the AFL-CIO headquarters to blast the Clinton plan. Workers and management united against the government-environmentalist alliance.

For the time being, however, the radical environmentalist movement holds the edge, having framed the debate in terms of "protecting" versus "destroying" the environment. As a result, in 1996 as many as ninety-one House Republicans—members of the first GOP-controlled House in forty years—were voting with Democrats on environmental issues. A poll found that 55 percent of GOP voters did not trust their party to "protect the environment," and the Clinton administration plan to "protect" the Everglades by putting a tax on sugar, taking thousands of agricultural acres out of production, and throwing thousands of people out of work, was considered a political winner.

One item on the Republican agenda which got stalled was the proposed revision of the Endangered Species Act (ESA), a key law that has served to implement the antigrowth agenda of the greens. Already, more than five hundred plants and animals are on the list, and four thousand candidates await listing. Simple math tells you that if one owl can virtually shut down an entire industry in the Northwest, four thousand of these critters can go a long way toward shutting down the entire economy.

In the case of the owl, the truth is that logging could have proceeded at 1980s levels. Despite propaganda to the contrary, our forests were growing faster than they were being cut. But, the president bowed to those who have misled the public by talking about old trees—"old growth"—and cute owls.

The old trees—mostly Douglas Firs—will die because of disease, drought, insects, or forest fires unless they're cut down. But, the radicals would rather see them die—even decay on the ground—than be harvested for human benefit. In fact, in July 1992, more than thirty people were arrested for cutting Northwest timber that had been blown down. They were threatened with six months in jail and/or a five hundred-dollar fine.

The radicals claim that the owls can only survive in "old growth" forests. But, Dixie Lee Ray pointed out in her book *Environmental Overkill* that "the biological needs of Spotted Owls are few. They need a place to nest and lay eggs, and enough trees to provide cover, but open enough so they can fly after and capture suitable prey. For food, the owl prefers rodents; woods rats and brush rabbits are favorites. Spotted Owls—Northern or California or Mexican—can survive wherever these conditions exist; the age of the forest is of no consequence."

On an international basis, the environmentalists have become experts at sounding the alarm about alleged dangers that supposedly threaten the entire planet. Their villain in many cases is the use of energy. This is why they are so committed to higher and higher taxes. Their stated objective is to drastically reduce our use of energy—the lifeblood of a modern, industrial economy.

The environmentalists have been so successful that it is considered politically incorrect these days to believe that global warming is a natural phenomenon that doesn't present an immediate threat to man's life on earth. You can still occasionally hear, see, or read about this view in the major media. But, if Jessica

Mathews has her way, it will be increasingly branded as the viewpoint of a few extremists and may eventually be totally suppressed. Mathews, a senior fellow of the Council on Foreign Relations and a regular columnist for the *Washington Post*, has written a column criticizing those editors and producers who, in the name of balance, give time and attention to those who question or doubt the theory that global warming is such a major threat that we have to make major changes in the American way of life.

It is amazing that a newspaper like the *Post*, supposedly devoted to the right-to-know, would publish a column like Mathews's. What Mathews called a "false controversy" is a real debate that should go further in educating the American people about the real agenda of the radical environmentalists. They don't want to protect the environment so much as they want to limit industrial progress, the source of the so-called greenhouse gases that they claim are causing the warming.

If the issue were as cut-and-dried as Mathews suggests, the proponents of the theory wouldn't have to resort to false claims and phony statistics. The *New York Times*, for example, published a sensational story based on preliminary data showing that 1995 was the "Hottest Year on Record." That would seem to support the global warming theory. But, the data used by the *Times* were incomplete; the information was only through November. December turned out to be a very cold month. Compared with a ten-year average for the same month, the temperature over much of the Northern hemisphere plummeted by almost 1.3 degrees in December. This was the largest one-month drop since 1979, when researchers started using satellites to gather the data.

Rather than admit that this information contradicted the-sky-is-falling environmentalists, the *Washington Post* put it this way: "This seemingly paradoxical finding is a reminder of the enormous complexities and uncertainties still connected with efforts to understand the global climate." Translation: they don't know what they're talking about.

The same goes for *Newsweek* magazine, whose 22 January 1996 edition hit the newsstands as much of the East coast was digging out from under a major snowstorm. The cover story carried the headline "The Hot Zone. Blizzards, Floods & Hurricanes: Blame Global Warming." This time the theory was that extremes in temperature reflected the phenomenon of global warming. Inside, however, the story said, "Last week's blizzard can't be blamed on the warming world. No storm or drought or heat wave ever can be so neatly diagnosed."

In fact, there's no evidence at all that the weather is more extreme and destructive. A George C. Marshall Institute report issued in April 1995 found no evidence of an increase in tornadoes and hurricanes as temperatures increase. On the contrary, it is cold—not warmth—which is associated with greater storminess.

The report found that although some global warming has occurred, it cannot be blamed on human or industrial activity, as the media imply, and the increase has only been half a degree over the last hundred years. Further, most of this increase occurred before 1940—that is, before most of the carbon dioxide caused by human industrial activity was released into the atmosphere. That means the warming is probably a natural phenomenon.

The Marshall Institute findings were released by Dr. Sallie Baliunas, a Harvard astrophysicist and chair of the Marshall Institute Science Advisory Board. The evidence from the study suggests it would be far wiser to collect more facts before implementing measures that could prove extremely costly to the economy and have no impact on the "problem" at all. But, that doesn't fit into the agenda of the environmental movement or the U.N.

Another popular environmental scare in recent years has been the claim that the ozone layer is developing a big hole, leaving us vulnerable to all kinds of threats to human health. But, a new organization called the Advancement of Sound Science Coalition points out it is already costing ninety million Americans eight hundred dollars each to modify or replace the cooling element in car air-conditioning systems that the scaremongers blame for creating the ozone hole. Yet, the coalition notes that "scientists now believe the ozone layer may repair itself, even without this expensive new regulation."

Another popular scare campaign involves chemicals in the environment. A new book titled *Our Stolen Future* makes the claim that exposure to synthetic chemicals is threatening the endocrine systems of people, destroying their balance of hormones, and impairing the ability of humans to reproduce. The catchy phrase "gender benders" has been invented to capture the essence of the alleged problem.

When those behind the scare held a news conference at the National Press Club to announce their findings, their publicity agent was the notorious Fenton Communications, the same public relations firm which represented Communist Nicaragua and the Salvadoran

Communist guerrillas and which helped orchestrate a national scare campaign over chemicals on apples. This scare resulted in apple growers losing hundreds of millions of dollars before the truth finally got out.

The Competitive Enterprise Institute was quick to rebut the "gender benders" scare campaign by issuing two excellent reports. One, titled *Rachel's Folly*, made the case that new restrictions on chemical use could actually harm human health by inhibiting the production of cancer-fighting fruits and vegetables or making them more expensive. The other, *Nature's Hormone Factory*, pointed out that nature itself produces chemicals that have the potential to disrupt endocrine systems and that these naturally occurring substances are far more prevalent than synthetic chemicals.

Moreover, synthetic chemicals are absolutely essential. These chemicals, in the form of pesticides and genetically engineered additives, make it possible to engage in high-yield agriculture. The entire story is told in Dennis T. Avery's excellent book *Saving the Planet with Pesticides and Plastics*. Avery, director of the Center for Global Food Issues at the Hudson Institute, argues convincingly that by promoting high-yield agriculture, conservatives actually conserve the environment better than the self-styled environmentalists.

The explanation for this lies in the fact that the liberals who claim to be proenvironment are actually promoting farming methods that result in very low yields. The only way, under these circumstances, to expand yields is to plow down millions of square miles of additional wildlands, thereby destroying the wild species which inhabit them and undermining the stated purpose of the environmentalists.

In addition, Avery points out that, at its current yields, organic farming "cannot possibly support the world's population without inducing unprecedented global famine." Faced with such an outcome, the radical environmentalist dream (or nightmare) makes "sense"—to dramatically reduce the human population and relegate the remaining people to isolated areas. Of course, such a course cannot be pursued painlessly. Many will die.

By contrast, high-tech and high-yield farming not only saves land and wildlife, Avery notes that it "reduces human cancer risks by providing inexpensive, attractive produce year-round; conserves our supplies of fresh water; saves our forests, including the crucial rain forests; and—lest we forget—feeds vastly increasing numbers of people while using fewer resources."

Avery focuses on the restrictions on logging in the Pacific Northwest as an example of how the liberals exacerbate the problem they claim to be concerned about. "The U.S. has much of the world's most sustainable crop and forestland," he points out. "Our farm and forest products should increasingly be exported to ease the pressure on forests in the tropics, which harbor most of the world's species. But to 'save' a Spotted Owl that wasn't endangered, liberals shut down logging on big tracts of our fastest-growing forests. Now the world's wood is being cut from tropical forests."

Avery has some advice for conservatives (and Republicans) on the environmental issue: don't spend so much time on conservation issues talking about jobs and property rights. Instead, discuss how the radical environmentalists are moving the planet toward an environmental catastrophe.

The key question—whether human beings are going to survive—depends on whether we are going to exploit our natural resources and our science and technology to provide for a rising standard of living for our people. Seen in this light, proposals for global taxes on energy will make the situation far worse by making it more expensive to produce and raise the products we need.

In fact, it can be persuasively argued that we need a drastic reduction in tax rates. This would enable American agriculture to provide even cheaper products for the domestic and international markets. But, this would not play into the hands of those who want the power to manage human affairs by redistributing the wealth of the world.

In combatting the global tax agenda, we have to explain to the American people how our standard of living has been brought to this point and why international taxes, especially a carbon tax, would devastate our society.

Fredric C. Olds, who specializes in energy communications, says we must return to the beginning:

> When the pilgrims came here 376 years ago, this country was literally forests and rivers, plains, deserts, mountains. There were no cities, no manufacturing, no electric lights, no telephones, no roads. It was a wilderness, and the people came here on their small sailing vessels, and they built their new homeland.
>
> From the first landings in 1620, it took the new settlers only 155 years to reach the point where they felt strong enough to declare themselves a nation with the Declaration of Independence.

At that time, this country still was very much an undeveloped nation—well below the standards of the advanced nations of the world. . . . During the next hundred years or so, the U.S. caught up with and surpassed the other industrial nations of the world. By the 1950s and 60s we, with just 5 percent of the population of the world, were producing and using 1/3 of all the energy being produced and used in the world of 4 billion people.

At that time, we owned 80 to 90 percent of all the significant technology in the world. We developed it. We owned it. We were the largest food exporter. We produced 25 to 30 percent of all the world's goods and services.

We were able to do this because people were free to find and develop and use the resources that were here in this country, and because they were ingenious and they were persistent and they were industrious. And because they produced electricity.[12]

As a result, Olds adds, if a global carbon tax ever gets implemented, the U.S. will by far pay the highest price because our electric society is dependent on the carbon fuels—coal, oil, and gas. Higher energy costs mean more expensive goods and services, leading to fewer of them produced and purchased. Our standard of living will decline but government will grow larger.

Perhaps this is not an accident.

Endnotes

1. World Resources. *A Guide to the Global Environment. The Urban Environment, 1996–97*, an official publication of Habitat II. The United Nations Conference on Human Settlements, June 1996, a joint publication by the World Resources Institute, the United Nations Environment Program, the United Nations Development Program, the World Bank (New York: Oxford University Press, 1996), 89.

2. Jeffrey Laurenti, *National Taxpayers, International Organizations. Sharing the Burden of Financing the United Nations* (New York: United Nations Association), 43.

3. "Renowned Speaker to Address Annual Meeting," *The U.N. Vision* (May/June 1994).

4. James Gustave Speth, Address on the Occasion of the Launch of the 1994 *Human Development Report,* 1 June 1994.

5. *Human Development Report 1994* (New York: Oxford University Press, 1994), 5.

6. Ibid., 9.

7. "A Call to Action: Summary of *Our Global Neighborhood*, the report of the Commission on Global Governance," (Geneva, 1995), 14.

8. Ibid., 217.

9. Ibid.

10. *State of the World, A Worldwatch Institute Report on Progress Toward a Sustainable Society* (New York: W.W. Norton & Company, 1993), 155.

11. Hilary F. French, *Partnership for the Planet: An Environmental Agenda for the United Nations* (Worldwatch Institute, July 1995), 56–57.

12. Fredric C. Olds, "The Electric Society Develops," made available to author.

Slave Labor

An extraordinary book was published in 1995 by a former reporter for *Forbes* magazine, Steven Solomon, in which he urged adoption of a global tax on international currency transactions and the formation of a "world economic directorate" to manage the economies of the nations of the world. Solomon claimed that his book was an inside look at how "unelected central bankers" are running the "global economy."

The book contains much valuable information about the behind-the-scenes operations of international bankers. But, it also serves as an argument for giving international bureaucrats even more power over world affairs. It is shocking but extremely revealing that a journalist of his prominence is on board the global tax bandwagon. It is not unreasonable to suggest that Solomon, who interviewed many of the big money men in the world today, is reflecting their views in pushing global taxes.

Entitled *The Confidence Game* (Simon & Schuster), the book cheered the hearts of those at the U.N. pushing these controversial tax-raising schemes, and it proves, once and for all, that concern about such a

tax being imposed on the world is not at all mis-
placed. In the book, Solomon proposes a version of
the tax which could bring in an amazing $13 trillion
a year.

"Such great sums," he says in the book, "could be
used to pay the cost of administering new financial
regulations. Some could be turned over to the Basel
club [i.e., central bankers] to pursue interventions to
stabilize currencies and to carry out lender-of-last-
resort missions. Some could finance the World Bank
for economic development, or an IMF that might be
restructured to evolve into a world central bank and
seat of a genuine world economic directorate."

In a footnote, Solomon acknowledged that his proposal is a variation of the "Tobin tax" on international
currency transactions proposed by economist James
Tobin and pushed under the auspices of the U.N.

In a review of the book for *The American Enterprise* magazine, John McClaughry describes Solomon's
proposal and commented, "This is the New World
Order with a vengeance." In arguing against this proposal, McClaughry points out that international currency transactions reflect the assets of people "who are
consciously shipping it around the world in search of
market opportunities, low tax rates, and productive
efficiency. Their responsibility is to live with the risks
they incur without expectation of government rescues
carried out at the expense of innocent taxpayers."

But, as the Solomon book indicates, the lure of
additional billions or trillions of dollars for the U.N.
and other international agencies may be too much to
ignore.

How would they do it? Any financial "crisis" could
serve as an excuse to push this tax, on the ground that

the international currency markets need the "stability" that regulation and taxes would supposedly provide. The tax would be marketed as an attack on "rich" investors who would, in reality, include the managers of the mutual funds and pension plans of ordinary Americans.

International taxes could be implemented under the cover of a "global crisis" of some sort, in which national governments or international agencies are "forced" to act. In this regard, the influential *Washington Post* has published an article about how the "international money markets could trigger a major financial crisis they might not be able to control." Concern about this was attributed to high-level Clinton administration officials, Federal Reserve officials, and "top Wall Street financiers."

At the end of the article, after several proposals for controlling this problem were discussed, the issue of the Tobin tax was brought up. E. Gerald Corrigan of Goldman Sachs, the former president of the New York Federal Reserve Bank, was said to have a "reservation" about the Tobin tax as "one way to reduce volatility in markets." Corrigan said, "Maybe a tax would be a good idea, but it literally would have to be universal. Besides, for a lot of these transactions you would have to have a really stiff price to change behavior. I don't think it would work. There is no chance of getting universality. . . . It's a very, very, very difficult problem to get your arms around."[1]

Leaving aside the possibility of universality, the U.N. has vigorously promoted such a tax. In the fall of 1994, in advance of the March 1995 U.N.-sponsored World Summit for Social Development, United Nations Development Program (UNDP) administrator James Gustave Speth endorsed it, saying that "a global human security fund" should be established, financed from "global fees such as the 'Tobin tax' on speculative movements of international funds."[2] The 1994 *Human Development Report*, issued by Speth's UNDP, was explicit in this regard, saying that "global taxation may become necessary" to "achieve the goals of global human security" and that one of the "promising new sources" of revenue includes "a small transaction tax on speculative international movements of foreign exchange funds.[3]

The 1994 *Human Development Report* went further, saying that "a tax on the international movements of speculative capital suggested by James Tobin, winner of the Nobel Prize for Economics, . . . could raise $150 billion a year."[4] The report featured an article by Tobin, winner of the 1981 Nobel Prize for Economics, who outlined his proposal and said it could produce revenues of *$1.5 trillion a year.*

> An international uniform tax would be levied on spot transactions in foreign exchange. . . . The revenue potential is immense, over $1.5 trillion a year for the 0.5% tax. . . . It is appropriate that the proceeds of an international tax be devoted to international purposes and be placed at the disposal of international institutions.[5]

The difference between the $1.5 trillion proposed by Tobin and the $13 trillion suggested by Solomon is easy to explain. Once a "small" tax is introduced, it could easily be increased. It could also start far smaller, in order not to unnecessarily alarm people.

At the World Summit for Social Development, proposals for global taxes were seriously offered and debated. One of the leading proponents was France's then president, Socialist Francois Mitterand. The *New York Times* reported, "He supported a proposal to tax speculative international currency transactions as [a] way of raising money for development. . . . President Mitterand . . . said he had no illusions about the difficulty of establishing a tax on financial transactions. But he challenged the audience of more than 115 government leaders to make a real commitment."[6]

Similarly, the *Washington Post* noted that the "Tobin tax" was offered and debated at the U.N. event:

> Another idea, proposed by James Tobin, an American who won the Nobel Prize for economics in 1981, called for a tax on speculative currency transfers to raise funds for development aid. A tax on short-term currency deals as small as 0.05 percent, U.N. officials say, could raise as much as $150 billion a year and produce the added benefit of discouraging disruptive financial speculation.[7]

Following up, the UNDP's 1995 *Human Development Report* referred to the ongoing "global human development debate" having led to "concrete policy proposals" on the tax ideas. It added that these include

> finding new sources of funding for global human security, such as the 'Tobin Tax' on international speculative movements of currency or internationally tradable permits for global emissions. At the recent World Summit for Social Development, proposals such as the 20:20 compact [a proposal for international financial assistance to poor countries] and the Tobin tax attracted widespread interest from many quarters.[8]

The report didn't explain the nature of this "widespread interest." But, it is beyond doubt that officials of the UNDP are extremely interested in and actively promoting the concept. Moreover, there is evidence that the UNDP facilitated discussions at the World Summit for Social Development on this topic. This was revealed by Alan F. Kay, a commissioner of a group called the Global Commission to Fund the United Nations, which is dedicated to "researching all feasible ways of funding the United Nations in addition to improving the collection of dues and assessments from member states."[9] Kay discussed what went on behind the scenes at the U.N. conference when he made an appearance at the National Assembly on the United States and the United Nations, a pro-U.N. group. This group, incidentally, in a "draft declaration" for consideration by delegates to the event, proposed a "serious exploration of alternative funding sources" for the U.N. Kay said that, "with the cooperation of UNDP and others in the U.N.," he promoted these plans.

As noted earlier, the Global Commission to Fund the United Nations issued its own report, entitled *The United Nations at Fifty: Policy and Financing Alternatives*, published as the March 1995 issue of *Futures: The Journal of Forecasting, Planning and Policy*. A news release summarizing its proposals urged establishment of "a 'Global Securities and Exchange Commission' to bring order and investor confidence back into roiling capital markets—while providing innovative funding sources for the United Nations." It added that "most relevant to today's financial crises, a levy of at least .001 % on international currency transactions" could bring in needed revenue.[10]

The commission, one of several private groups pushing global taxes, is a 501(c)3 not-for-profit corporation whose "Secretariat," currently a director and associate director, is based in Washington, D.C. There are fifty-seven commissioners and nineteen members of the commission's advisory council. It is significant that current and former U.N. officials have played a key role in this commission. These include Bella Abzug, a former member of Congress and prominent participant in the U.N.-sponsored Fourth World Conference on Women in Beijing, China; Mahbub ul Haq, special advisor to the UNDP administrator and former finance minister of Pakistan; Inge Kaul, director of the Human Development Report Office of the UNDP; Robert Muller, former assistant secretary general of the United Nations for Economic Affairs; Marie Angelique Savane, director, Africa Division, United Nations Population Fund; Brian Urquhart, former U.N. undersecretary general for Special Political Affairs; Ruben Mendez, professor of economics, Yale University, and advisor to the UNDP; and Dr. Dharam Ghai, director, U.N. Research Institute for Social Development.

One of the authors contributing an article to the commission's special edition of *Futures* was Inge Kaul of the UNDP. Her article was titled "Beyond Financing: Giving the United Nations Power of the Purse." In order to rectify the "present financial constraint on UN activities," the article proposed "to shift the burden of financing the UN from national to global sources—by introducing charges for the use of global commons or levies on international activities such as trade and foreign currency transactions."[11]

Other articles in this special edition of *Futures* devoted to global taxes were written by Harland Cleveland, a former official of the U.N. Relief and Rehabilitation Administration; Erskine Childers, former senior adviser to the U.N. director-general for Development and International Economic Cooperation; Hans d'Orville, former assistant secretary, UNDP Governing Council and Dragoljub Najman, former assistant secretary general of the United Nations Educational, Scientific, and Cultural Organization (UNESCO); and Ruben Mendez, a historian with the UNDP.

Mendez is a key link between the Global Commission to Fund the United Nations and another group pushing global taxes called the Commission on Global Governance. Mendez, a former senior UNDP official, wrote an article endorsing global taxes in *Choices*, the official organ of the UNDP. In the April 1995 issue, Mendez proposed a variation of the Tobin tax, urging that a "Foreign Currency Exchange" be established as an agency of the U.N. to "generate vast revenues" for the world body. Mendez declared, "It is time to make an intellectual quantum leap, and to look beyond the nation-state for new, innovative and independent transnational sources of funds."[12]

This new proposal stemmed from Mendez's fear that the Tobin tax is unworkable because "formidable obstacles stand in its way." He explained, "Foreign exchange transactions are often loose and informal. They leave no 'paper trail' by which they can be monitored and taxed." By contrast, his Foreign Currency Exchange (FXE) would behave like foreign securities exchanges already do, only on a less expensive basis by offering lower rates. The FXE, he says, would be a

"publicly-owned entity" run by the U.N. At a 1 percent rate for fees and commissions, it could generate
$840 million a day, he said.[13]

In his *Choices* article, Mendez noted that he had
previously endorsed the Tobin tax in a report in 1993
to the Commission on Global Governance. This organization is probably the most important "private"
group pushing global taxes, although it received significant financing from various governments. Funding
for its work has come from the governments of the
Netherlands, Norway, Sweden, Canada, Denmark,
India, Indonesia, and Switzerland. The government
of Japan arranged for funds for the commission from
"two United Nations trust funds." In addition, the
MacArthur Foundation, the Carnegie Corporation,
and the Ford Foundation in the U.S. provided financial assistance.[14]

Of particular significance is the fact that the executive director of this commission, Peter Hansen,
went on to become undersecretary general for Humanitarian Affairs at the U.N. In this capacity, he
gave a presentation on "Alternative Sources of Financing the UN System" at the National Assembly on
the United Nations and the U.S. He spoke of the
potential of new "money raising approaches" for the
U.N. being "very, very persuasive" and favorably cited
the proposal for the Tobin tax on international currency transactions. "It is time to take some action
here," he declared.[15]

The commission itself held a series of meetings,
beginning in September 1992 and ending in October
1994, which produced a volume entitled *Our Global
Neighborhood* in 1995. The commission included
twenty-eight members drawn from twenty-six coun-

tries. The U.S. members were Barber Conable, former
Republican congressman, and Adele Simmons, presi-
dent of the MacArthur Foundation. Other members
included Oscar Arias, former president of Costa Rica;
Hongkoo Lee, prime minister of Korea; Brian
Urquhart, former U.N. official; and Yuli Vorontsov,
Russian ambassador to the United States and foreign
policy adviser to President Yeltsin.

The summary of the final document declared, "An
international tax on foreign currency transactions
should be explored as one option" to bring in more
revenue.[16]

Despite the appeal of the Tobin tax as "a revenue
enhancer" for the U.N., the premier pro-U.N. lobbying group, the United Nations Association, declared
that today "the opposition is also likely to be
formidable. . . . In the current political atmosphere, at
least in the United States, one may expect considerable resistance to any 'new taxes,' especially for a distant global organization like the U.N."

International environmentalists, while preferring
taxes on energy, nevertheless also support an international currency tax. In its 1993 report, *Progress Toward a Sustainable Society*, Hilary French endorsed a
"levy" on "international flows of money." She explained,

> To discourage currency speculation, Nobel-lau-
> reate James Tobin has suggested that a 0.5-
> percent tax be placed on foreign exchange trans-
> actions, which Tobin calculates would have the
> side-benefit of raising more than $1.5 trillion
> annually. But even a far smaller levy would
> raise sizable funds. For instance a tax of just
> 0.05 percent on current daily currency transac-
> tions would raise $150 billion annually—more

than 75 times the recent replenishment of GEF
[Global Environment Facility].[17]

Similarly, the antipoverty group Oxfam came out
in support of a currency tax, saying that "an international tax on currency speculation could serve the dual
purpose of providing resources for development and
deterring a financial activity which is deeply destabi-
lizing for all countries."[18] The World Federalist Association, a group promoting "world federation," has
also endorsed "taxes on international financial transactions."[19]

It is important to note that a key international
money manipulator, George Soros, whose financial
transactions would be subjected to the Tobin tax, is a
big backer of the U.N. He was the keynote speaker at
the May 1995 conference of the Business Council for
the U.N.

Soros was also a big backer of the Bosnia peace
agreement, whereby U.N.-affiliated international institutions such as the IMF took control of the country's
central bank. But, Bosnia isn't the only example of
how the power of global money, working its way
through international agencies, can affect the fate of
nations.

Another example is the Mexican bailout, in which
the leadership of both political parties participated. It
was a $48.8 billion package designed to bail out inves-
tors burned by the fall in value of the Mexican peso
and the threat of a Mexican government default on
peso-dominated bonds. These investors included
Goldman Sachs, the number one underwriter of
Mexican stocks and bonds in the U.S. and European
markets for 1992 through 1994. Goldman Sachs has
had a longtime relationship with Clinton. In the 1980s,

it helped to underwrite $400 million in bonds for the Arkansas Development Finance Authority. Goldman Sachs co-chairman Robert Rubin and Mack McLarty, who became White House counselor under Clinton, were good friends. Rubin, worth an estimated $100 million, and his wife contributed $275,000 to the Democratic National Committee in 1992.

After the election, they were rewarded for their financial contributions. Rubin joined the Clinton cabinet, and Kenneth Brody, a Goldman Sachs general partner, was appointed by Clinton as chairman of the Export-Import Bank. Goldman Sachs also defended Clinton against his mounting legal troubles. A Washington lobbyist for Goldman Sachs, Michael Berman, had raised money to defray the Clintons' legal expenses stemming from the Whitewater investigation and Paula Jones's sexual harassment lawsuit.

In the book *The Buying of the President*, Charles Lewis explained the seedy details surrounding the Mexican deal:

> Rubin spearheaded Goldman's move into Mexico, and the firm had steered billions of dollars into that merging market over the years. The peso crisis of 1993–94 came to a head just as Rubin was becoming treasury secretary. His one-year recusal from dealing in matters affecting Goldman Sachs had ended. By helping Mexico to make good on its commitment to bondholders, the $20 billion U.S. portion of the bailout was viewed by some as a publicly-financed insurance policy for Rubin and Goldman Sachs, along with other large investment houses and banks that were highly exposed in Mexico. Rubin was a partner in the

firm and could be civilly liable for claims by investors. Mexico has already used the bailout money to pay back investment banks.

If the bailout was not a guarantee, the investment community was further reassured by the "Framework Agreement for Mexican Economic Stabilization," signed by Treasury Secretary Rubin and the Mexican Ministry of Finance on February 21, 1995. The document gave the Department of the Treasury "the right to distribute, in such manner and in such order of priority as it deems appropriate" the Mexican export revenues it now controls. In other words, Robert Rubin had the power to grant first right of payment to whomever he chooses, including the holders of Mexican bonds purchased from Goldman Sachs.

The $20 billion, of course, was just part of the deal. This is the money that came directly from the Federal Reserve and a little-known Treasury Department account called the Exchange Stabilization Fund (ESF). The IMF furnished another $17.8 billion, and $12 billion came from other sources.

Moreover, the deal was based solely on President Clinton's "executive authority." Where does the president get the authority to send tax dollars abroad and to arrange additional financing through the IMF? In a report produced for the Citizens United Foundation, Michael Boos charged that the use of the ESF to bail out the peso violated "the spirit, intent and letter of the ESF statute." He pointed out that the bailout called for extension of ESF credit for periods of three to five years, although the statute does not authorize the extension of credit or loan guarantees for longer than twelve months.

Rather than challenge the administration's action, the Republican congressional leadership went along with the scheme, enabling Clinton to claim and use more power than he was legally and constitutionally entitled to. This meant that the Republicans lost a crucial opportunity to explain to the American people how U.S. law has been manipulated to assist international organizations, foreign governments, and special interests.

The ESF grew out of the "emergency powers" legislation arising out of the 1930s depression. Originally, it was designed to stabilize the exchange value of the dollar. In 1945, Boos notes, as part of the Bretton Woods Agreements Act, which authorized U.S. membership in the IMF, the ESF was made part of the permanent laws of the U.S. In 1976, amendments were passed to the Bretton Woods Agreements Act, authorizing the use of the ESF to extend credit where such credit is "necessary to and consistent with United States obligations in the International Monetary Fund." This represents a perversion of the original purposes of the IMF.

The idea behind the IMF was to avoid the kind of post-World War I economic collapse that was blamed for World War II. The IMF was supposed to be a temporary source of funds for nations needing to balance their books. The World Bank, another Bretton Woods institution, was supposed to provide development loans. Another institution, the proposed International Trade Organization, failed for lack of support.

Today, these organizations, including the newly created World Trade Organization (WTO), constitute an important aspect of what some call the New

World Order. They have generally failed to assist development in the Third World, but have succeeded in draining a lot of wealth from the U.S., giving international bureaucrats tremendous power over world events.

"IMF Tells U.S. to Boost Rates" was the headline over a 19 July 1994 article in *Investor's Business Daily*. This is typical of how the IMF has assumed the power to tell other nations, including the U.S., how to manage their economic affairs. IMF Chief Michel Camdessus "suggested that the U.S. needs to raise interest rates in order to keep its economic expansion going," the article said.

In fact, in another sign that international agencies are interfering with American sovereignty, the IMF also warned Congress not to cut taxes for the American people. In its World Economic Outlook study, the IMF urged lawmakers to reduce the fiscal deficit before cutting taxes. It advocated a program which "postponed the introduction of significant tax cuts until substantial progress toward a balanced budget" has been achieved.

The critical issue is why the IMF claims the right to meddle in internal U.S. affairs. If the IMF were simply a private, Socialist think tank, that would be one thing. But, it is actually a U.S. taxpayer-financed international body that claims the authority to manage the world economy. So, we, as citizens, are paying the salaries of bureaucrats who are in effect lobbying to keep our taxes high.

This, apparently, is the price of being a player in the "global economy." It is not unreasonable to speculate that at some point in the future our own massive debt may prompt the U.S. to seek financial aid from these international agencies, putting us even further under their control.

The IMF threat helps illustrate the awesome power of these international agencies. The dramatic confrontations between the Clinton administration and the Republican Congress in 1995 over balancing the budget may have led some people to think that all of the economic decisions affecting our nation are made in Washington, D.C. In fact, many are made elsewhere.

But, Mexico wasn't the only country in need of a taxpayer-financed bailout. In a last-ditch effort to save the presidency of Boris Yeltsin, the International Monetary Fund (IMF) announced a $10 billion "loan" to Russia in the spring of 1995. More than $300 million a month was pumped into Russia beginning in April so that Yeltsin could try to buy votes before the 16 June presidential election.

We were led to believe there were significant differences between Yeltsin and his leading opponent, Communist Gennady Zyuganov. However, though a "non-Communist," Yeltsin had installed as his foreign minister Yevgeny Primakov, the former head of a branch of the Soviet KGB. Moreover, the U.S. business and financial establishment was prepared to deal with whomever won the election. Columnist Robert Novak reported that pro-U.N. billionaire businessman George Soros was observed having breakfast with Zyuganov at a February 1995 meeting of the World Economic Forum. Novak said Zyuganov was trying "to reassure international investors—such as Soros— by promising to create a 'climate of confidence' that their funds will be safe in Russia."

For these businessmen, the U.N. and its affiliated institutions represent a form of regulation of the world economy that works to their benefit. It doesn't really matter who is in charge of nation-states as long as they play along with big business, big banks, and the U.N.

The leadership of both political parties, under the influence of big business, supported the creation of the WTO, in which the U.S. has only one vote among 120 countries, pays 20 percent of the bill, and has no veto power to stop anti-American decisions which are made in secret. The WTO manages international trade and is an integral part of the U.N. system today.

Leading the charge against the WTO during the presidential campaign, Patrick J. Buchanan said about U.S. leaders, "What are they doing surrendering our sovereignty to a World Trade Organization where we get one vote out of 120 and Fidel Castro can cancel America's vote?" Nevertheless, the Alliance for GATT Now, a lobbying group that promoted the WTO, represented some of the nation's leading business organizations, including the Business Roundtable, National Association of Manufacturers, and the U.S. Chamber of Commerce.

In January of 1995, when the WTO ruled in favor of Venezuela and Brazil over the U.S. in a case involving foreign oil, only Pat Buchanan among all the presidential hopefuls spoke out against it. Why were all the other candidates silent about a cause involving the erosion of our national sovereignty? The answer, again, has got to be money. The Business Council for the U.N. (BCUN) is a virtual "Who's Who" of the international business community. Members include Archer Daniels Midland Company, the Rockefeller Group, Chemical/Chase Manhattan Bank, and IBM. These companies or their officers pour tremendous amounts of money into the political process.

In 1992, a big business-funded organization called the Committee for Economic Development (CED) issued a report calling for increased U.S. support for international trade agreements and "global economic institutions" such as the United Nations, the World Bank, and IMF. In fact, it urged that the IMF be strengthened and that the U.S. increase its support of the U.N. Population Fund and International Planned Parenthood. A CED Subcommittee on a Global Economic Strategy for the United States actually formulated this report and was headed by Bank America chairman A.W. Clausen, a former president of the World Bank.

The U.N.'s role in the global economy is critical. An official U.N. document explains, "Within the framework of the General Agreement on Tariffs and Trade (GATT), which in January 1995 was replaced by the World Trade Organization (WTO), the United Nations has supported trade liberalization that will increase economic development opportunities for developing countries."

From the U.N.'s anti-American perspective, "free trade" is designed to transfer America's productive capacity to the rest of the world. America's foreign trade deficit approached $200 billion in 1995 and could reach $250 billion by 1997. Much of this trade imbalance is with Japan, but $40 billion is with Communist China, where slave labor is reported. Yet, the leadership of both major political parties favored extending Most Favored Nation (MFN) trading status to Communist China.

By extending MFN, Republicans and Democrats were turning a blind eye and deaf ear to human rights champion Harry Wu, a Chinese dissident who became an American citizen. Wu, who survived nineteen years in China's "laogai" system of slave labor camps, had charged that the World Bank over the last ten year years had invested more than $100 million in projects in the Xinjiang Autonomous region of China, an area where a quasi-military organization runs prison camp labor.

After the World Bank issued a report claiming it works only with the "civilian" arm of the organization in "anti-poverty" work, Wu responded, "They accepted Chinese lies and then they repeated them." Wu called for an independent investigation, saying "The World Bank cannot investigate itself."

China's use of slave labor—and the indifference of U.S. and business leaders to the practice—is very troubling in the context of understanding our place in the global economy. It appears the "global economy" is a phrase that actually refers to forcing American workers to compete with those who get little or nothing in the rest of the world. The inevitable result is a decline in our own standard of living.

From the viewpoint of multinational corporations and Wall Street financial interests, which have no allegiance to the national interest, "free trade" maximizes the ability to transfer jobs and money across borders. They are not entirely to blame for this. Liberal, leftist, and environmentalist groups, working through largely Democratic Congresses, have made it too difficult to make money here by piling high taxes and cumbersome regulations on American businesses.

There was a time when the interests of U.S.-based big businesses coincided with those of average Americans. From 1950 to the mid-1970s, millions of Americans found good jobs with these firms. But, with the development of what is called the "international labor market," these corporations found that they could produce the same goods and services for a much cheaper price. This has resulted in massive corporate "downsizing," in the name of facing "global competition."

Figures show that annualized weekly wages peaked in 1972 and are now below 1956 levels, even while chief executive officers of major companies continue pulling down multimillion dollar salaries. For example, Louis Gerstner, chief executive officer of IBM, made $2,626,000 a year while laying off sixty thousand. Gerstner is a prominent member of the Business Council for the United Nations.

Another example is Walter V. Shipley, chairman and chief executive officer of Chemical/Chase Manhattan. His salary was $2,496,154 while he put twelve thousand people out of work. He, too, is a prominent member of the BCUN.

BCUN members also include Capital Cities/ABC, the New York Times Company, the Turner Broadcasting System, NBC, and Rupert Murdoch's News America Corp. This means that the "global media" have no interest in telling the full truth about what is happening to the American standard of living under U.N.-managed trade deals because they profit from the very same arrangements.

This is an issue involving our sovereignty. America is not in control of our destiny because the country has been sold out to foreign interests, international agencies, multinationals, and their agents. It is not "isolationism" to call attention to this problem; it is the highest form of patriotism.

The problem for Pat Buchanan, who made this a critical issue in the campaign, is that he did not have the resources to adequately compete in a political process dominated by big money. He stayed at budget hotels and took advantage of "free media"—doing interviews on radio talk shows. Oliver North, who ran for the Senate from Virginia, commented that Buchanan had "clearly alienated the GOP's money. It is great to have the image of someone fighting the big moneyed interests of the party, but tough to actually be doing so."

The issue that enabled Buchanan to make gains in the Republican primaries was not "protectionism" per se but the issue of who is going to be protected. Buchanan wanted to protect American workers against cheap and slave labor. The political party establishments want to protect the big businesses and the big investment houses which provide them with financial contributions. This is why both parties arranged the taxpayer bailout of a corrupt regime in Mexico that was in hock to Wall Street interests such as Goldman Sachs.

One patron of both party establishments is Dwayne O. Andreas, chairman of Archer Daniels Midland (ADM), the huge agribusiness conglomerate which had net sales in fiscal year 1994 exceeding $11 billion. Andreas has served as a member of the board of trustees of the BCUN.

In 1992, Andreas and his company contributed $270,000 to help Clinton and the Democratic party capture the White House. But, during the presidency of Republican George Bush, who openly embraced the New World Order, Andreas funneled more than $1.1 million to the Republican National Committee.

ADM poured tens of thousands of dollars into Senator Dole's senate and presidential campaigns, as well as his leadership PAC and think tank. Dole's relationship with Andreas earned him the nickname, "The Senator from ADM."

However, showing his heart really was with Clinton, Andreas predicted the lifting of the U.S. trade embargo of Communist Cuba during the next Clinton administration. "Common sense will lead to the end of the embargo in the next administration," he said. "Nixon opened up China, Bush went to Russia, and Clinton can do the same thing with this tiny little island." This "tiny little island" was a base for Soviet nuclear warheads targeted on American cities, a center for Communist subversion in the Western hemisphere, and even the State Department acknowledges that Cuba continues to facilitate drug trafficking into the U.S.

But, for people like Andreas, it is just another business opportunity. This is what's wrong with big business today and why Buchanan struck such a chord with the American people. This is the New World Order in action; hard-pressed American taxpayers being forced to subsidize multinational entities who support America's enemies. And, now they want global taxes to make us pay more.

All of this, of course, is carefully packaged as "free trade," and even some conservatives were highly critical of Buchanan, saying he had broken with the "free trade" policies of one president he served, Ronald Reagan.

However, the truth is that the Reagan administration got extremely tough with Japan during the 1980s, pursuing a policy that gradually opened up the Japanese market. This remarkable story is detailed in the report *Roadmap for Results: Trade Policy, Technology and American Competitiveness*, produced by the Council on Competitiveness.

The Reagan administration never permitted "free trade" in the sense of letting Japan dump products on the U.S. market. On the contrary, the Reagan administration encouraged U.S. industry in filing an unfair trade case against Japan. As a result, a U.S.-Japan Semiconductor Arrangement was signed in 1986, and in 1987 the Reagan administration applied sanctions worth $300 million for noncompliance with this deal. But, even this wasn't enough. In 1991 and 1992, new agreements were reached with Japan to increase American access to the global and Japanese market.

It was under the Reagan administration in 1987 that the Semiconductor Manufacturing Technology Consortium (SEMATECH) was created. This is a joint industry-government funded research consortium. Some conservatives deride this as an "industrial policy" and antifree trade, but the evidence shows that it was pursued under the Reagan administration and that it was ultimately successful.

Moreover, this wasn't the only area where such a policy was pursued. Virtually the same thing occurred in the communications equipment industry. Beginning in 1984, the Reagan administration and U.S. industry began working together to open up the Japanese market to American cellular telephones. In 1984, an antidumping action was filed against Japan, followed by discussions on the issue between President Reagan and Japanese Prime Minister Nakasone. One year later, antidumping duties were formally imposed on Japan. It wasn't until 1989 that Japan finally agreed to reallocate communications frequencies to allow access for U.S. companies.

There are many other such cases, demonstrating that when U.S. companies were faced with unfair competition, the Reagan administration did not hesitate to join with American industry against foreign regimes that exploited our market, still the largest in the world. The result was that billions of dollars of revenue and tens of thousands of American jobs were saved.

But, now, under the terms of the WTO, our options are even more limited. Our vote gets cancelled out by Castro.

Endnotes

1. John M. Berry and Clay Chandler, "Volatile Money Pool Worries U.S. Officials," *Washington Post*, 17 April 1995.

2. James Gustave Speth, Address on the Occasion of the Launch of the 1994 *Human Development Report*, 1 June 1994.

3. *Human Development Report 1994* (New York: Oxford University Press, 1994), 5.

4. Ibid., 9.

5. Ibid., 70.

6. Barbara Crossette, "As World Poverty Talks Open, A Plea From France's President," *New York Times*, 12 March 1995, 4.

7. William Drozdiak, "Rich, Poor Meet at Summit, And Go Their Separate Ways," *Washington Post*, 12 March 1995, A15.

8. *Human Development Report 1995* (New York: Oxford University Press, 1995), 120.

9. "Global Commission to Fund the United Nations Releases First Report," 6 March 1995, news release, 2.

10. Ibid.

11. *Futures: The Journal of Forecasting, Planning and Policy*, vol. 27, no. 2 (March 1995).

12. Ruben Mendez, "Harnessing the Global Currency Market for the Global Common Good," *Choices* (April 1995): 16.

13. Ibid., 17.

14. *Our Global Neighborhood, The Report of the Commission on Global Governance* (New York: Oxford University Press, 1995), 376.

15. Peter Hansen, remarks at National Assembly on the United States and the United Nations, "Alternative Sources of Financing the UN System," audio tape, recorded 1 September 1995.

16. *Our Global Neighborhood. The Basic Vision* (Geneva: The Commission on Global Governance, 1995), 45.

17. Hilary F. French, *Partnership for the Planet: An Environmental Agenda for the United Nations* (Worldwatch Institute, July 1995), 56–57.

18. *The Oxfam Poverty Report* (Oxfam, 1995), 221.

19. "U.N. Funding" leaflet, Campaign for Global Change, World Federalist Association, 1995.

War Crimes

7

Allies of the U.N. seem to be quite open about what they want global taxes for. They cite such nice-sounding causes as environmental programs, peace-keeping, and "family planning." However, global taxes would almost certainly have to underwrite the U.N.'s rapidly expanding operations in the judicial realm.

The most dangerous new U.N.-sponsored institution may well be the International Criminal Court, which would require billions in dollars in global tax revenues. "If the United States and other countries are serious about a New World Order, orderly procedures for establishing laws and the capability for enforcing laws via courts and 'police' would seem to be the serious heart of the matter," declared Wendell Gordon in his book *The United Nations at the Crossroads of Reform.*

As a revenue source, Gordon suggested that multinational corporations might agree to an international corporate income tax if the money could be used to finance an international legal system to protect their interests and reduce international "chaos" in the Third World where they conduct business.

He explained, "An effectively working business community requires the existence of impartial courts and meaningful police power to enforce the sanctity of contract. If corporations can obtain the rule of law in exchange for the international corporate income tax, they will have struck a good bargain."

It is unclear at this point whether a global corporate income tax will be the preferred global tax and whether the system would be exclusively geared toward protecting the interests of multinational corporations. Gordon's book appeared as the U.N.'s International Criminal Tribunal for the former Yugoslavia was getting underway, and he expressed the hope that it too could lead to "a permanent and respected police force and a judicial system capable of trying individuals." Indeed, it is this tribunal that has led U.N. supporters to believe that an International Criminal Court (ICC) is within their grasp.

If this tribunal is perceived as a "success," the U.N. and its allies are convinced that the ICC will become a reality and that revenue for international prosecutions of all kinds will be forthcoming. The ICC could imprison and prosecute individuals for "crimes against humanity" and other vague offenses, potentially including "colonialism," "environmental crimes," or even "hate crimes." The judges could come from Cuba or North Korea. Nevertheless, the concept has been endorsed by such groups as the American Bar Association and the American Society for International Law and could soon be a reality.

The court could also be used to go after those who don't pay their "fair share" of global taxes. Gordon himself noted that, in order to collect an international tax on multinational corporations, the U.N. would

have to have the "police power" to "make such collec-
tions effective." This would come through an enhanced
U.N. judicial arm—the authority to arrest, prosecute,
and imprison people on a worldwide basis.

Currently, the U.N. has an International Court of
Justice, also known as the World Court, whose rul-
ings are mere opinions. The prospect of the U.N.
having a criminal court with compulsory jurisdiction—
and an independent source of revenue for the world
body—would complete the process of the U.N. becoming a full-fledged world state.

Of course, the U.N. is not packaging the ICC in
the terms used by Gordon because they sound too
scary. Instead, the ICC is being packaged attractively
as an effort to bring international outlaws, terrorists,
and war criminals to justice. Under these circumstances,
it's hard for people—most especially the politicians in
Washington, D.C.—to declare their opposition to such
a judicial proceeding. However, if these politicians
have any feeling left for American sovereignty, or even
of their own places in history, they will quickly realize
that the ICC could also hear politically charged cases
against American political and military leaders and
that the cases could be decided by representatives of
Communist countries or terrorist regimes. In other
words, American political and military leaders could
end up serving time in U.N.-run prisons.

The prospect of the U.N. having an ICC was
highlighted in an article in the March/April 1996 issue of *Foreign Affairs*, where U.N. Secretary General
Boutros Boutros-Ghali himself pointed out that the
main U.N. body, the General Assembly, was "now
considering" the establishment of a permanent ICC.

The process appeared to be moving quickly. Prior
to the November 1996 presidential elections, a meeting of the U.N.'s Preparatory Committee on the Establishment of the International Criminal Court was
held 25 March through 12 April and reportedly produced remarkable progress. A 12 August through 30
August session was supposed to draft the final text.
Some observers thought that the Clinton administration might even try to get a treaty establishing the
ICC through the Senate before the 1996 election.

President Clinton had himself strongly endorsed
the ICC in a speech in October of 1995 at the dedi-
cation of the Thomas J. Dodd Research Center at the
University of Connecticut. Dodd's liberal son, Sen.
Christopher Dodd (D-Conn.), a co-chairman of the
Democratic National Committee, has been the leading cheerleader for the ICC. Trying to portray the
court in the best possible light, Dodd had suggested
that it could have been useful in prosecuting the PLO
terrorists who staged the 1985 terrorist attack on the
Achille Lauro cruise ship and killed American citizen
Leon Klinghoffer.

However, the prospect of the ICC being used exclusively to target enemies of Israel or the United
States was not readily apparent. The Israeli military
attacks on Lebanon in April of 1996 could also be fair
game for the ICC. In fact, Israeli military officers—
even political leaders—could be prosecuted by such a
court. A possible case against Israel was buttressed by
a United Nations report charging that the Israeli attack which killed more than one hundred refugees in
a U.N. camp in southern Lebanon did not appear to
be a mistake, as the Israeli government had insisted.
U.N. Secretary General Boutros-Ghali's embrace of

this report led to intense criticism of him from Israel and the Clinton administration.

The U.S. Department of Defense (DOD) was said to be opposed to the court, arguing that the ICC could prosecute American military officers for actions that take the lives of civilians in military operations abroad. Officially, however, DOD did not object to the ICC.

A Democratic takeover of the U.S. Senate in November 1996 and President Clinton's reelection would virtually guarantee ratification of the ICC treaty. However, it is also quite possible that a GOP-controlled Senate could pass the proposal because of the perceived need to appear tough on human rights violators. Sen. Arlen Specter (R-Pa.), a former prosecutor, is one of the most prominent advocates of the new world body. Another supporter is Sen. James Jeffords (R-Vt.).

Robert Dole's position on the ICC was not immediately known, although he was considered a possible backer. But, even if he were opposed, the Democrats would only have to pick up a dozen or so GOP senators in order to pass the ICC treaty with a required two-thirds vote of those senators present.

In the House, some of the strongest support for the ICC comes from Republicans. Rep. Jim Leach, for example, is a prominent backer of the ICC. Leach, a member of the House since 1976, served as president of Parliamentarians for Global Action, a "worldwide network of national legislators" which lobbies for more U.N. power and influence over international affairs. The group is funded by big liberal foundations, various governments, and the U.N. itself. Leach also served as co-chair of the U.S. Commission on

Improving the Effectiveness of the U.N., a body established by Congress.

Other known members or supporters of Global Action included Representatives Connie Morella, Patricia Schroeder, and Gary Ackerman, and Senators Tom Harkin, Paul Simon, and James Jeffords.

One of Global Action's most important programs was in the area of international law, where it promoted the establishment of the U.N. Tribunals for the Former Yugoslavia and Rwanda, the ICC, and "the advancement of the principle of individual accountability under international law."

But, Global Action was part of a much larger group, the NGO Coalition for an International Criminal Court, a network that has been working to support the creation of the ICC. Other members of the coalition are Amnesty International, the Baha'ia International Community, the (Jimmy) Carter Center, Equality Now, Human Rights Watch, the International Commission of Jurists, the Lawyers Committee for Human Rights, the Quaker U.N. Office, and the World Federalist Movement.

Sen. Jesse Helms, as chairman of the Senate Foreign Relations Committee, played his familiar role, leading the opposition to the ICC. In a 1994 speech calling it "very unwise and very dangerous," he raised the specter of such a court prosecuting Americans for colonialism or "environmental crimes" before judges from North Korea and Cuba. John Bolton, a former assistant secretary of state, agreed that the ICC is "a lousy idea" that could easily be turned against the U.S. He compares it to the U.N. Human Rights Commission, a group which has been manipulated by human rights violators around the world such as Cuba into a forum for condemning the U.S. record on human rights.

Though liberal groups are said to be disappointed that the Clinton administration wanted the U.N. Security Council (where the U.S. has a veto) to exercise control over the court's jurisdiction, Bolton said the U.S. veto is seldom used and that he could easily foresee the ICC becoming another anti-American propaganda vehicle.

How would it work? Herbert Romerstein, an expert on Communist disinformation and intelligence activities, noted that in the 1940s, a Communist-front group known as the Civil Rights Congress filed a petition with the U.N. charging the U.S. with "genocide" for its treatment of blacks. Under the ICC, black racist Louis Farrakhan or one of his backers, a country such as Libya or Iraq, could bring "genocide" charges against the U.S. over treatment of blacks or Indians. The list of possible charges against the U.S. is endless. And, even if the U.S. had the power to veto such cases, they would still be of immense propaganda value to America's enemies. One could easily envision left-wing groups staging mock hearings on "war crimes" or "crimes against humanity" involving U.S. leaders past or present.

The ICC is considered a logical successor to the International Criminal Tribunals for the Former Yugoslavia and Rwanda, established to prosecute "war criminals" from those conflicts. Not wanting to appear soft on human rights violations, most members of the U.S. Congress—Democrats and Republicans alike—have gone along with this effort. The bipartisan support for the Yugoslavia court in particular convinced ICC supporters that the time is right for cre-

ating the ICC and that Republicans could be convinced to go along with it.

However, the creation of the Yugoslavia court was
itself a power grab and sets a dangerous precedent. It
was established without the benefit of a treaty by the
U.N. Security Council when it decided that chapter 7
of the U.N. charter, authorizing the deployment of
U.N. military forces, also gave the world body the
ability to arrest, prosecute, and jail individuals.

As the U.N. itself admitted in an unofficial back-
ground paper, "Normally, such a Tribunal would be
established by treaty rather than by the Security Council. The Secretary-General, however, pointed out that
such an approach would require 'considerable time'
and that 'there could be no guarantee that ratification
will be received from those States which should be
parties to the treaty if it is to be truly effective.'"

The Center for U.N. Reform Education, a pro-
U.N. group, admitted that the creation of this tribunal was "unprecedented" and that article 29 of the
charter was used in an unusual manner to establish
the tribunal as a "subsidiary organ" of the U.N. In an
understatement, the group said that the Security
Council's creation of the court "appears on the surface
to be a rather liberal interpretation of the traditional
peace and security mandate. As such, it represents one
more expansion of the Council's jurisdiction."

In other words, the U.N. broke its own charter in
order to justify expansion of its own powers. Is this
the kind of entity we want arresting, prosecuting, and
throwing people in jail?

On the basis of this shaky foundation, the tribunal has engaged in some extraordinary actions, such as
engineering the capture and arrest of one Bosnian

Serb in Germany, Dusko Tadic, and charging him with "war crimes" such as rape and "abuse." In a story about the case, Marlise Simons of the *New York Times* indicated that the defense team had a point in drawing attention to the "vagueness of the court's rules, definitions and standards of evidence."

The American Bar Association, which supports the tribunal, nevertheless concedes that its operations fall far short of what the U.S. justice system is supposed to require. Writing in the *ABA Journal*, James Podgers noted that jury trials are the norm in common-law systems in the U.S., Britain, Canada, and Australia. In the Yugoslavia tribunal, however, judges find the defendant guilty or not guilty. In the U.S., judges are supposed to be neutral. The judges in the Yugoslavia tribunal are not; they can play an active role in eliciting testimony from witnesses. In the U.S., the Sixth Amendment to the Constitution requires that the accused be confronted by his accuser. However, judges in the Yugoslavia tribunal can allow some witnesses to remain anonymous, even to defendants and their lawyers. Moreover, the tribunal announced in April of 1996 that it had issued about a half-dozen secret indictments and that the identities of those named in them would not be revealed until the suspects were arrested.

Disregarding all of this, feminists cheered the operation of the tribunal because of its emphasis on rape and other "gender-related acts of violence" as war crimes, as the *ABA Journal* put it.

Incredibly, despite the seriousness of most of the crimes under discussion, the Yugoslavia tribunal was not entitled to hand down the ultimate penalty of death for atrocities that were supposed to be gruesome by historical standards. Like most liberals, the U.N. is against the death penalty.

A larger question involved whether the conflict in the former Yugoslavia even qualified as worthy of this kind of attention. Was it a civil war or did it have an international dimension that required U.N. intervention? And, why do these crimes require an international tribunal anyway? If rapes or assaults were committed, why not prosecute them as ordinary street crimes?

In this case, the prosecutors were trying to portray the indicted Serbs as agents of a grand conspiracy mounted from Serbia that used "ethnic cleansing" as part of a state-organized policy. This tactic reflected the propaganda that got the U.S. involved in the conflict in the first place. The war in the former Yugoslavia was frequently referred to as a "holocaust," similar to what the Nazis did against the Jews, involving "death camps" and so forth. In reality, as Richard Cohen of the *Washington Post* acknowledged, "there's little doubt that the Serbs have behaved abominably. But so, too, on occasion, have the Muslims." He said a comparison to the Nazi holocaust "exaggerates the crimes of the Serbs and diminishes those of the Nazis—and, of course, obscures suffering elsewhere."

However, the propaganda served its purpose, eventually laying the groundwork for U.S. and NATO intervention in the region and the holding of trials by the tribunal. There was intensive pressure to use American troops to arrest those charged by the tribunal.

By May of 1996, the tribunal had indicted fifty-seven people—forty-three Bosnian Serbs, three Serbians, eight Bosnian Croats, and three Bosnian

Muslims. At this time, however, only three suspects were in custody. They were housed at a special twenty-four-cell wing of Scheveningen prison near the Hague.

But, the overreaching nature of the tribunal's activities finally got to be too much to bear, even for some liberals. The tribunal's indictment of a Serb general for allegedly ordering military attacks on civilian targets was strongly criticized by *Washington Post* deputy foreign editor Edward Cody, who noted that similar charges could have been brought against "a long list of respected leaders around the world," including President Harry Truman for the Hiroshima bombing and Winston Churchill for the bombing of Dresden during World War II.

Offering a similar criticism, conservative legal scholar Bruce Fein added, "The entire concept of crimes against humanity or war crimes is too elastic and its inevitable political manipulation too arbitrary to satisfy the fundamental imperative that the law should warn before it strikes." Fein called the dubious indictment of the Serb general "compelling evidence" against the creation of the ICC.

Another argument against the ICC is sheer cost. The costs associated with the Yugoslav and Rwanda tribunals have already reached into the tens of millions of dollars, although the *ABA Journal* complained that they "continue to encounter difficulties in obtaining appropriate and timely funding from the United Nations." This is another way of saying that they want and need more money. Global taxes are an obvious source.

Bureaucracies have a way of growing. As of April 1996, 311 people of thirty-six different nationalities were working for the tribunal, and the costs were

escalating. For the first year, the U.N. put the cost at
$32.7 million. In the meantime, other groups were
contributing funds. The Open Society Institute of
George Soros provided $105,000 and the Rockefeller
Foundation $50,000. For its part, the U.S. was paying
about one-third of the costs. The U.S. State Department said that, in the time period of 1994–1995, the
U.S. provided $9.5 million for the court in the form
of outright grants and computers and software. However, continuing its practice of raiding federal agencies
to benefit the U.N., the Clinton administration also
provided personnel to the effort. This included two
prosecutors and five investigators from the Department of Defense, six prosecutors and three investigators from the Department of Justice, and five foreign
service officers from the Department of State.

The costs associated with the establishment and
operation of the ICC, a "permanent" U.N. arm, are
not known. It would require a bureaucracy, investigators, a police force to arrest targeted individuals, and
a prison system. However, U.N. Secretary General
Boutros-Ghali had the answer to this problem: his
Foreign Affairs article included another call for global
taxes on international currency transactions, energy,
and international travel. He predicted that a source of
"automatic" funds for the U.N. would be a reality by
the next century—just four years away.

The other serious problem with the holding of
these tribunals and the establishment of an ICC is the
sheer hypocrisy of the entire spectacle. For example,
one of the judges of the Yugoslavia tribunal is from
Communist China, a dictatorship where the Communist rulers have murdered tens of millions but have
escaped prosecution. Like the Yugoslavia court, the

judges for the ICC would be drawn from all U.N. members, including China, Cuba, North Korea, Libya, Iraq, and Iran.

Of all of these, Cuba has been the most persistent threat to the U.S. It has been an outpost for Soviet nuclear missiles targeted at the U.S. and has exported drugs and terrorism to surrounding countries, including the U.S. Yet, Castro, who never stood for a free election, is a hero of the U.N. and received a thunderous standing ovation when he addressed the U.N. General Assembly in October of 1995.

In El Salvador, where Cuba intervened on the side of Communist terrorists, the U.N. claims to have performed a mediating role by establishing a process that led to "peace" and an eventual amnesty for both sides in the conflict. However, the results didn't provide any justice for Col. Ed Pickett (retired), whose son David was murdered in cold blood by the Communists after his military helicopter was shot down in El Salvador in 1991. Ed Pickett has spent subsequent years trying to get the U.N. and the U.S. State Department interested in beginning the process of apprehending his son's killers.

Russia, which still supports Cuba despite the breakup of the old Soviet Union, is a member in good standing of the U.N. despite the brutal war it waged against rebels in the Chechen Republic, where bombing campaigns killed tens of thousands of innocent women and children.

Russia, now occupying the Soviet seat on the U.N. Security Council, may be the greatest terrorist nation the world has ever known. It helped spark World War II through the partitioning with Germany of Poland in 1939 and the Hitler-Stalin pact between the leaders of both nations.

During the war, the Russians massacred twenty thousand Polish officers in Katyn Forest. In 1950, just five years after the formation of the U.N., the Soviet Union helped North Korea launch the Korean War, costing America fifty-four thousand dead and one hundred thousand casualties. The Communist Chinese entered the war on the side of the North Koreans.

In the Vietnam War, where Communist forces were equipped by the Soviet Union and China, fifty-eight thousand Americans lost their lives.

Despite this record, there is never any consideration given to holding the leaders of Communist China or Russia accountable for war crimes. This is because the U.N. is essentially a pawn of these two nations. Nothing happens without their approval.

The additional absurdity involved in the notion of the U.N. prosecuting "war crimes" lies in the fact that U.N. Secretary General Kurt Waldheim was himself guilty of participating in war crimes during World War II and yet was picked as secretary general, later left the organization, and was never prosecuted. In fact, he left with an eighty thousand dollar a year pension. Waldheim, a citizen of Austria, was U.N. secretary general from 1972–1981.

It's true that, officially, Waldheim's Nazi ties were not known at the time of his U.N. service. But, Eli M. Rosenbaum's book, *Betrayal*, makes a convincing case that the Communists were aware of his Nazi links and used the information to compromise Waldheim into serving their interests. Rosenbaum, now the head of the Nazi-hunting Office of Special Investigations in the Justice Department, called Waldheim a longtime Soviet asset whose tenure was characterized by a massive increase in Soviet agents operating at the world body. Rosenbaum noted that Waldheim even traveled to Moscow in 1977 and presented Soviet dictator Leonid Brezhnev with the gold United Nations peace medal.[1]

U.N. hypocrisy on the issue of "war crimes" is also evident in the failure to prosecute all the Japanese war criminals from World War II. This is especially ironic because the U.N. tribunals and the ICC are supposed to be updated versions of the Nuremberg tribunals, which prosecuted, convicted, and executed war criminals from that conflict. Yet, the evidence is overwhelming that some of the worst war criminals were made exempt from war-crimes prosecution. One who was spared was Lt. Gen. Shiro Ishii, the architect of these crimes, who supervised biological experiments on American POWs. Evidence unearthed by Washington, D.C.-based researcher Greg Rodriquez indicates that Gen. Douglas MacArthur, commander of the Allied Powers in Japan, provided immunity from prosecution to Ishii and his cohorts in exchange for their germ warfare data. Rodriquez's father was a POW in one of the camps where the experiments were conducted.

At the time, it was thought that the information might be useful in countering the Soviets, who were developing their own weapons of mass destruction. Indeed, the U.S. plan seemed to be to recast Japan as a U.S. ally, a strategic bulwark against the Soviets. "Even as we met on the battlefield," declared one U.S. State Department document, "plans were being developed at the State Department for a new relationship— one between friends, partners and allies."[2]

One story, citing declassified U.S. military documents, noted, "Unlike Germans who were tried for their experimentation on humans, the Japanese germ-warfare researchers became some of Japan's most prominent citizens—university presidents, heads of medical centers. Lt. Col. Ryoichi Naito, Ishii's right-hand man, founded Green Cross, one of Japan's top pharmaceutical companies."[3]

Today, fifty years after the fact, there is no reason why these Japanese war criminals should not be pursued in the same way Nazis have been hunted down. However, a major complicating factor is Japan's bid for a permanent seat on the U.N. Security Council, where it would be in a position to pay more of the U.N.'s bills. This is not an insignificant issue. Until the U.N. implements a global tax scheme, so-called voluntary contributions from member-states are the main source of revenue. Japan and Germany—which also wants a permanent U.N. Security Council seat—are the logical places to go in the meantime.

The Heritage Foundation has pointed out that any plan to expand the number of seats on the U.N. Security Council would further dilute the influence of the United States in the world body. However, if a case could be made for allowing either Germany or Japan on the Security Council, Germany would be a far better candidate. The Center for Civilian Internee Rights, a group representing allied victims of the Japanese, says, "Germany has atoned for their World War II crimes. . . . They have paid out more than 90 billion marks in compensation/reparations and apologizes almost daily. They are continuing to pay compensation to the survivors until the survivors are all dead. Their textbooks fully cover their World War II misdeeds and the vast majority of the German people are repentant of the Nazi actions." By contrast, Japan has failed to do this.

The Center for Civilian Internee Rights, whose executive director is Gil Hair, wants to block Japan's acquisition of the U.N. seat until Japan financially compensates its victims and issues an official apology. The group has filed a claim against Japan at the U.N. Human Rights Commission.

But, the allure of Japan's increasing involvement in and support for the U.N. may be used to justify a continuing effort to ignore Japan's war crimes history. Lt. Gen. Richard Myers, who served as head of the forty-seven thousand U.S. troops in Japan, was quoted in *Pacific Stars & Stripes* as saying that Japan should be taking a more active military role in U.N. peacekeeping operations and that the country has already had "tremendous successes" in its first steps toward such a role. He pointed to Japan's participation in U.N. peacekeeping operations in Cambodia, Mozambique, Rwanda, and the Golan Heights.

A new book on Japanese and American perspectives on U.N. peacekeeping even examines the potential for Japanese-American "cooperation" in U.N. military activities in the years ahead.[4]

In terms of the so-called regular budget of the U.N., Japan is already the number two contributor behind the U.S. While the U.S. contributes 25 percent, Japan provides 12.5 percent. This percentage, which is supposed to reflect a country's share of the world economy, will have to go up. In fact, some experts say that Japan's economy will surpass the U.S. economy by the year 2000.

It is significant that the work of the Commission on Global Governance, which endorsed a series of global taxes, was supported by two U.N. Trust Funds "established by Japan" and that the U.N. University co-hosted a public symposium with the commission in Tokyo. The U.N. University was established with $100 million from the government of Japan.

Largely for financial reasons, Japan figures to play a more prominent role in the U.N. in the future. Its war crimes will be conveniently forgotten, making a mockery of the world body's commitment to "justice."

Endnotes

1. Eli M. Rosenbaum, with William Hoffer, *Betrayal. The Untold Story of the Kurt Waldheim Investigation and Cover-up* (New York: St. Martin's Press, 1993), 70.

2. Robert M. Kimmitt, *The U.S. and Japan: Defining Our Global Partnership*, Current Policy No. 1221.

3. Ken McLaughlin, "Evidence of Atrocities Ignored. Germ Warfare: U.S. May Have Known Its POWs were Experimented upon," *San Jose Mercury News*, 13 August 1995, 1A.

4. Selig S. Harrison & Masashi Nishihara, ed., *UN Peacekeeping. Japanese and American Perspectives* (Carnegie Endowment for International Peace, 1995).

The New State Religion

In promoting global taxes, the U.N. and its supporters claim the additional revenue is needed for such things as environmental protection and military peacekeeping. But, there is a great deal of evidence suggesting that international taxes would also help subsidize a world religion or a world church. This is because the United Nations has religious roots and to a great extent already promotes and underwrites its own brand of religious expression. This aspect of U.N. affairs has received little attention. Critics of the U.N. frequently speak of it as a godless institution, which is true in the sense that its charter does not refer to a Creator as a source of our human rights.

But, the facts speak for themselves. The U.N. Environmental Program (UNEP), which American taxpayers are forced to subsidize to the tune of $100 million a year, actually functions much like a state church. It vigorously promotes the concept of an "Environmental Sabbath," in which the earth is glorified in place of God, going so far as to establish a North American Environmental Sabbath Planning Committee. UNEP also published a report entitled *Ethics &*

Agenda 21, a reference to the "plan of action" adopted by the 1992 Earth Summit. Most of the report is devoted to providing religious reasons for implementing the environmentalist agenda.

Why the resort to religion? In the introduction to the report, Dr. Noel J. Brown, director of UNEP, refers to the "economic debate" over how much it will cost to restore the earth and puts the cost at an incredible $600 billion a year. He also talks about the "social debate" over this effort. But, what is lacking, he says, is "a much clearer sense of the ethical and moral issues posed by Agenda 21." He concludes, "We are, after all, earth's only moral creatures, and to be true to our nature we need to give the fullest moral expression to the way we treat the earth."

In other words, the only way we're going to force the nations of the world, primarily the United States, to cough up hundreds of billions of dollars a year is to make this environmental movement into a religious crusade, making people feel bad if they don't fork over the big bucks. Guilt is always an effective way to accomplish this.

Incredibly, American taxpayers are already helping make this a reality. The Presidio National Park in San Francisco, a former U.S. military garrison managed by the National Park Service, has emerged as the world's headquarters for this religious campaign, which seems to be evolving into the establishment of a world religion. Established as a national park to benefit American citizens, the Presidio has been transformed into the location of the Gorbachev Foundation, a think tank created by the former Soviet President Mikhail Gorbachev. Though an outcast in his own country, Gorbachev enjoys very close relations with many leading citizens in the U.S. who think he has given up on communism.

Officially, the Gorbachev Foundation is a "tenant" of the Presidio. A Park Service employee explains that the foundation is allowed to operate there because it is regarded as a "non-profit" group which is "not affiliated with any political ideology."

But, this is laughable. Gorbachev's ideology is a clever mixture of green and red. He has masqueraded as a savior of mankind, trying to merge the concept of environmental protection with religious ideas. One of his close allies is Bishop William Swing, leader of the Episcopal Diocese of California, who wants a United Religions organization headquartered at the Presidio.

At his State of the World Forum in San Francisco in 1995, Gorbachev unveiled an "Earth Charter"—a sort of constitution for an emerging world government. This Earth Charter only makes sense in the context of giving a world government control over the planet in the name of saving the world's environment. This is their goal, and they will argue that it is necessary because of the calamity that they themselves have ushered in.

Appropriately enough, Gorbachev presided over perhaps the most environmentally irresponsible nation in history—the Soviet Union.

His latest project is the writing and acceptance of a Charter of Human Responsibilities, which was proposed during the May 1995 Summit of Religions and Conservation, held at Windsor Castle under the chairmanship of His Royal Highness, Prince Philip, Duke of Edinburgh. The Alliance of Religions and Conservation, which grew out of the summit, was awarded a U.N. special prize for helping to "reach untold millions world wide with a conservation message through religious channels." Nearly three thousand religious groups are said to be associated with it.

The Gorbachev Foundation says this charter will be implemented through "two proven networks"—the Alliance of Religions and Conservation and the State of the World Forum, those individuals and organizations working with Gorbachev. Gorbachev's October 1996 State of the World Forum was expected to attract over six hundred prominent individuals from fifty nations. His eventual goal is to complete the charter, have the State of the Forum adopt it, and then have one major organization per faith adopt it by the end of 1997. Eventually, the charter will be "officially disseminated through UN structures, with an eventual goal of establishing a Court of Human Responsibilities to whom individuals or groups can appeal," his literature says.

Though portrayed in terms of encompassing all faiths, a reporter for the *San Francisco Chronicle* described the tone of the October 1995 State of the World Forum as "unorthodox," noting that leaders of mainline Western religions were mostly absent. One of the speakers, Deepak Chopra, has since emerged as a major spiritual guru for many Americans, courtesy of the American taxpayer-financed Public Broadcasting Service (PBS), which has brought him into tens of millions of homes through his television programs.

One of his books, *The Way of the Wizard*, begins, "People want to know why I, who come from India, am so interested in wizards. My answer is this: in India we still believe that wizards exist. What is a wizard? Not simply someone who can perform magic but someone who can cause transformation."

Liberals who complain about government violating the "separation of church and state" have been noticeably silent about public television's seemingly endless promotion of Chopra, who has made a fortune dispensing "spiritual advice." His many programs on PBS have included one titled "Alchemy: The Art of Spiritual Transformation."

If Chopra were an evangelical Christian, the odds are that he wouldn't get the time of day from PBS. In fact, he'd probably be set up for a special investigation of his financial empire. An Associated Press story reports that Chopra has already made millions through books, audio tapes, TV appearances, and speeches.

Though a medical doctor by training, his appeal lies in using the teachings of Ayurveda, which are described as "the ancient science of healing" and "ancient wisdom" from India. He avoids traditional Christian teachings and embraces Eastern mystical religious concepts like "Karma." Indeed, he rarely mentions Christianity, except in terms which play down its uniqueness. For example, in an interview with a publication appropriately titled *Body, Spirit, Mind*, he insisted that every person has a "wizard" which leads to "God consciousness," which he also defined as "Christ consciousness."

In this state, Chopra claims people can "have an experiential knowledge of Divinity, perceiving God in a flower, in a tree, in a rainbow, in other beings." In another altered state he defines as "cosmic consciousness," he claims people become aware "that there is spirit in the world of matter." All of this sounds strikingly similar to the nature worship that seems to grip the radical environmentalist movement and people like Gorbachev.

Dubbed the "Hollywood Soul Man" and "guru to the stars," he's been an advisor to such personalities as ex-Beatle George Harrison, Olivia Newton-John, Michael Jackson, and Demi Moore. *Entertainment Weekly* reported that he taught Naomi Judd how to meditate, but that because she is a Christian, she decided to stick with prayer.

Perhaps because he enjoys backing from Hollywood, he's been accepted by the PBS crowd. The PBS station in Los Angeles, KCET, sponsors his programs for national distribution and sends out official press releases announcing his shows which feature quotations from the Upanishads, one of the ancient Hindu teachings.

The problem is not only taxpayer dollars going through PBS to promote his teachings, but the fact that Hindu theology is considered by most Christian thinkers to be primitive, heretical, or even blasphemous because Hinduism holds that God and man are ultimately one and the same. Christianity, by contrast, holds there is a gulf between man and God that is breached by Christ.

While Chopra spouted Eastern-style New Age mysticism to the American people through PBS, Clinton administration Secretary of the Interior Bruce Babbit was traveling the country delivering a speech entitled "Between the Flood and the Rainbow," in which he attacked his own Catholic upbringing and made environmental protection into a holy war.

One speech, delivered to the National Religious Partnership for the Environment and the American Association for the Advancement of Science in 1995, referred to nature as "sacred" and "holy" and claimed that "religious values remain at the heart of the Endangered Species Act." On the other hand, he was full of contempt for traditional Christianity, saying, "I learned my religious values through the Catholic Church, which, in that era, in that Judeo-Christian tradition, kept silent on our moral obligation to nature." Babbitt went on to credit the native American "priests of the snake clan" for "awakening" in him respect for the environment.

Babbitt's smear was denounced by the Catholic League for Religious and Civil Rights, which noted that appreciation and respect for nature has always been a part of the Catholic tradition and that the *Catechism of the Catholic Church* refers to the need for "moral" considerations in exploiting the earth's resources for human benefit. But, Babbitt's bashing of Catholics, though offensive, wasn't the central issue. Rep. Helen Chenoweth (R-Idaho) was more on target when she objected to the speech as an example of "a government-sponsored religion in America."

She explained, "This religion, a cloudy mixture of New Age mysticism, Native American folklore, and primitive Earth worship, is being promoted and enforced by the Clinton Administration in violation of our rights and freedoms." She said it was clear that Babbitt was attempting to regulate and enforce "his dream of utopia into reality" and that the key problem with government involvement in this "environmental religion" was that "non-believers face persecution."

But, Babbitt was simply echoing Vice President Gore, who had attended the U.N. Earth Summit and spoke at the Episcopal Cathedral of St. John the Divine, where he sermonized that "God is not separate from the earth." This theme was also highlighted in his book, *Earth in the Balance*.

Leading environmentalists also subscribe to this view. Chenoweth noted that Sierra Club director David Brower had been quoted as saying, "We are a kind of religion." Scientist James Lovelock authored a book about "Gaia," a reference to a supposed spirit of the earth, and said that Gaia was "a religious as well as a scientific concept."

Viewed in this context, the environmentalist drive for global taxes takes on a more sinister connotation. Since the environmentalists are some of the biggest boosters of global taxes, it is reasonable to assume that some of the increased revenues which go to U.N. environmental programs would also underwrite their religious activities. It is also not unreasonable to suggest that what the U.N. really wants to establish is a state—or world—religion, cloaked in the garb of environmental activism.

The evidence, in fact, is all around us, although the media portray this activity in the best possible light. Significant moves have already been made toward a world church. In 1990, more than 150 religious leaders from twelve faiths and forty nations met at the Princeton Theological Seminary in New Jersey, where they launched the World's Religions for the World's Children. It was organized by the World Conference on Religion and Peace and the United Nations Children's Fund (UNICEF). In 1993, the Parliament of Religions met in Chicago and issued a document entitled *Towards a Global Ethic*, with heavy environmental overtones.

It is interesting, to say the least, that those in America supposedly devoted to a strict separation of church and state have not seen fit to challenge the U.N.'s or even the Clinton administration's activities in the religious area. Their silence may have more to do with the content of the religious expression than the fact that government is involved in promoting it. Government support for traditional Christian teachings, which emphasize a personal God and a personal savior, Jesus Christ, are always discouraged by these organizations. By contrast, the U.N.'s religious activities, which obscure the uniqueness of the Christian faith, seem to be acceptable to them.

The U.N. Environmental Program's promotion of Environmental Sabbath activities are especially interesting. One of these documents explains,

> The Environmental Sabbath seeks to revitalize the teachings of each faith and tradition that bring respect and restoration to the creatures and the biosphere. It seeks to bring healing rest to Creation and each creature; it seeks to bring relief from relentless human pressing. It seeks peaceful times and places on earth; it seeks conditions that allow revitalizing Creation's sustaining processes and rejuvenating its creatures. The environmental Sabbath seeks rest for the Earth.

One document, intended for pastors of U.S. churches, advises that each congregation have a "special day," presumably a Sunday, set aside for the Environmental Sabbath. In a section of the document entitled "Suggestions for the Celebration," pastors are told, "Direct your congregation toward action: not only in church, but in the home, at school, in the political process. Be specific, mentioning local issues if possible." The document even includes prayers and music for the "celebration."

To be sure, the UNEP material includes references to the Christian faith. Indeed, a heading entitled "Scriptural Sources" cites various Bible verses meant to show "care for the earth," the "covenant," and "stewardship." Prayers reprinted in the document are drawn from Christianity, in addition to Buddhism, Hinduism, Judaism, Islam, native Americans, the Religious Society of Friends, and Baha'i.

However, it is apparent that the UNEP version of Christianity differs significantly from what most Christians are taught. One UNEP document, in a summary of "religious perspectives" on environmental issues, features a "Christian" viewpoint referring to "ecological sin," defined as "refusing to share with needy others—both other needy human beings and the needy natural world." This is an interesting concept. However, it has never been part of the Ten Commandments.

The effort to rewrite Christianity into some form of earth worship reflects the fact that Christ-centered religion does not fit in well with the other faiths that the U.N. wants to mold into some form of world religion or state church. The purpose of Christianity wasn't to save the earth but save people. In addition, Christianity is much different than the other religions because of the unique claims made by Jesus Christ and his self-identification with God the Father. Jesus said in the Gospel of John, chapter 14, verse 6, "I am the way, and the truth, and the life; no one comes to the Father but through me." In another passage, verse 9, Jesus said, "Whoever has seen me has seen the Father."

How does the U.N. deal with these claims? By ignoring or distorting them. Especially disturbing are the UNEP efforts to bring children into its religious environmental campaign by having them engage in Eastern religious practices such as meditation. One UNEP document includes a list of "games, activities and improvisations to save the earth" designed for children. An activity described as "Tree Span," recommends that children "gather 'round a beautiful tree. Look, listen and meditate upon it as long as you can." Children are advised to "experience the tree, for only by contemplating with a quiet mind can we fully experience and reverence nature."

The use of the term *reverence* is key. U.N.-style religion wants people to "reverence" nature, not God or Christ.

Another activity, called "Mount Olympus" and designed "for all students," entails this scenario:

> A family meeting of the gods or the Lords of The Universe is discussing the problems of the rogue Planet Earth. Your group is a delegation from Earth, come up to plead the case for human survival, but the gods are not convinced. They feel the long-term prospects for Earth are not good and are discussing drastic action: Burn them off with global warming? Send a disease to wipe them all out? Or try another messenger to teach human beings what they are doing wrong?

This reference to "another messenger" is a direct swipe at Christianity, implying that the message of Christ was not sufficient to save mankind. But, who might the other messenger be?

The answer may lie in an examination of a key nongovernmental organization represented at regular briefings of the U.N., a mysterious group called World

Goodwill. It is a program of the Lucis Trust, a member organization of the U.N.'s Economic and Social Council, which describes itself as "a non-profit world service organization dedicated to the establishment of right human relations through cooperation and caring. Its activities promote the education of the human mind towards recognition and practice of the spiritual principles and values upon which a stable and interdependent world society may be based."

Other than occasional advertisements in newspapers such as the *Washington Post* (from which the preceding quotation was taken), the Lucis Trust is probably an unknown entity to most people. Its officials are not familiar names. It creates the impression of being just another liberal, feel-good organization. In fact, it is something else entirely.

The Lucis Trust, incorporated in the U.S. in 1922 with offices in New York, England, and Switzerland, was reportedly originally known as the "Lucifer Trust." The term *Lucifer* refers to Satan, the archangel cast from heaven for leading a revolt of the angels against God. It literally means "light-bearer." Although it connotes evil to Christians, the term has a different meaning for people who believe that what Satan offered to human beings in the biblical Garden of Eden, knowledge of good and evil, is something which enables humanity to grow in its own development and awareness of God.

World Goodwill and Lucis Trust include many different references to Christianity in their literature, even quoting from the Bible and Jesus Christ. However, it stops far short of recognizing Jesus Christ as the only Son of God. It is also full of references to Eastern religious practices, such as meditation, and highlights the use of what it calls "esoteric teachings" and "occult science."

Both groups follow the writings of Alice A. Bailey, a disciple of Russian-born Madame Blavatsky, author of a book on New Age or occult Theosophy entitled *The Secret Doctrine*. Bailey, who claimed to receive telepathic instructions from Djwhal Khul, a Tibetan master, wrote books on meditation, telepathy, astrology, "esoteric healing," and "white magic." One of her books, *A Treatise on White Magic*, asserts that "man is essentially and inherently divine."

Equally significant, Bailey referred to the U.N. as "the hope of the world" and a "great field of experimentation" in which people undergo an "awakening" about their true nature. Bailey wrote about what Lucis Trust describes as "a subjective synthesis in humanity and of a telepathic interplay which will annihilate time."

World Goodwill distributes a pamphlet entitled "The United Nations: Entering the Global Age" and describes one of its objectives as "to support the work of the United Nations and its Specialized Agencies as the best hope for a united and peaceful world."[1] Another document, "The New World Religion," declares that "the concept of a world religion and the need for its emergence are widely desired and worked for. The fusion of faiths is now a field for discussion. Workers in the field of religion will formulate the universal platform of the new world religion." It further declares, "In the New World Religion the science of invocation and evocation will take the place of what we now call 'prayer' and 'worship.' "

World Goodwill also distributes a pamphlet outlining a mysterious "New Group of World Servers," described as the "Custodians of the Plan," the "inner spiritual government of the Planet."[2] One document is titled "Preparation for the Reappearance of the Christ," and the group talks openly about "the reappearance of the World Teacher—the Christ," who is "expected by millions, not only by those of Christian faith but by those of every faith who expect the Avatar under other names—the Lord Maitreya, Krishna, Messiah, Imam Mahdi and the Bodhisattva."

Moreover, the figure Maitreya is believed by some to exist today and live in London. Benjamin Creme, who is associated with Share International and the Tara Center, insists that Maitreya has a physical appearance but can appear and disappear through the power of thought alone.

Russell Chandler, an award-winning religion writer for the *Los Angeles Times*, says it's "naive" to think of the Lucis Trust "Plan" as a "present, organized conspiracy." He says, "Proof of this cannot be convincingly demonstrated."[3]

However, it's hardly necessary to prove the existence of a conspiracy, especially when these groups work openly through the U.N. What is lacking is any systematic effort to describe what they are doing and attempt to understand what it is they think they are accomplishing.

There are many knowledgeable observers who do think something strange is going on. One is Dr. Michael G. Zey, who, in his book *Seizing the Future*, describes the "New Age philosophy" as having a "profound international influence" around the world through such groups as the Esalen Institute, which sponsored and financed Boris Yeltsin's 1989 U.S. tour before he became Russian president. Zey asks, "Are the penetration of these networks into official circles the first step in a world government informed not by science and technology but by sorcery and witchcraft?"[4]

Critics might respond that since there's nothing scientific about sorcery, witchcraft, or telepathy, the entire New Age movement is nothing to be concerned about, only laughed at. Indeed, some of it is patently ridiculous. However, it is a fact that the U.S. intelligence community was avidly interested in paranormal phenomena. It started a program in the 1970s to investigate the application of one paranormal phenomenon—remote viewing, or the ability to describe locations one has not physically visited. The program involved the use of psychics—people supposedly with the ability to detect or affect things not using the normal five senses.

The American Institutes for Research, which reviewed the program, declared, "Even though a statistically significant effort has been observed in the laboratory, it remains unclear whether the existence of a paranormal phenomenon, remote viewing, has been demonstrated." Sen. Alphonse D'Amato said the program was kept alive because similar psychic research was being pursued by the Soviet Union, China and "some of our European allies."

If it's true that the intelligence community and the academics who reviewed its work cannot come to any firm conclusions, the possibility of paranormal activities cannot be dismissed out of hand. It is certainly a fact that some people believe they take place and that such practices can be facilitated by certain mental processes.

In this context, World Goodwill stages what it calls "The Great Invocation" in cooperation with the U.N.—a song or poem involving "spiritual energies"

that are "channeled" through the U.N. It ends with
the words, "Let Light and Love and Power restore
the Plan on Earth."

At the same time, the Lucis Trust advises its supporters and followers to engage in the practice of
"meditation at the full moon." A pamphlet explains
that a full moon "offers the greatest opportunity for
meditation—particularly in group formation—to be
used as a means of cooperation with the divine Plan
or Intention for our world."

All of this may strike some as bizarre or extreme.
If so, it is equally strange that the major liberal media
have not published stories about these practices. Reports of people meditating before a full moon would
be entertaining at the very least. However, these practices may not belong in the same category as "Elvis
Presley is alive" sightings. They may not be that laughable in the highest reaches of the U.N.

An examination of World Goodwill materials
demonstrates that their claims of working with the
U.N. are not laughable at all. Current or former U.N.
officials who have either spoken to the group or been
interviewed in its publications include Robert Muller,
former assistant secretary general of the U.N.; Jacques
Baudot, coordinator of the 1995 U.N. Summit for
Social Development; Erskine Childers, former senior
advisor to the U.N. director-general for Development
and International Economic Cooperation; and Henryk
J. Sokalski, coordinator for the U.N.'s International
Year of the Family project.

In their book *Spiritual Politics*, Corinne
McLaughlin and Gordon Davidson attempt to document the existence of a "Spiritual Government" operating behind the scenes of world events through the

U.N.[5] Davidson was associated with World Goodwill, and their book features an endorsement from Noel Brown, director of the UNEP.

They discuss a "meditation room" at the U.N., sometimes referred to as a "chapel." A photograph of this room, featured on the cover of William Norman Grigg's book *Freedom on the Altar*, shows it is bereft of any conventional religious symbols.[6] A group known as Friends of the Meditation Room is reported to meet regularly there. McLaughlin and Davidson write about its significance:

> The room is a place of quiet stillness and has been referred to as one of the holiest of holies on the planet, yet it is accessible to the public on request from the visitors lobby. It is the focus for the energies of a unified planet and humanity, and for right relations among all kingdoms of life. When Gordon worked for the UN for four years with World Goodwill, an NGO there, he meditated daily in this room and experienced a very powerful energy helping to support the synthesis of nations and the emergence of the Soul of humanity.[7]

They go on to write about the existence of spiritual entities involved with the U.N.:

> From the deeper perspective of the Ageless Wisdom, there are certain vast Beings of great Love and Light on an inner level whose energy can assist humanity only when there is a group consciousness and an energy field composed of the entire human family. One such Being, which could be called an Avatar of Synthesis, is said to focus energy on the United Nations General Assembly, to assist the efforts of hu-

manity in synthesizing the vast diversity of earth peoples and nations by strengthening a slowly growing will to unity. Delegates and staff who work in the energy field of the UN and are of goodwill speak of being profoundly changed by being there, of developing respect and compassion for all humanity by their exposure to the energies of human convergence focused there.[8]

McLaughlin and Davidson suggest that people start meditating on the U.N. as well as "Devas and angels"—the "invisible builders of all that we see in the world." These are described as "nature spirits." Through meditation, sometimes conducted while "lighting a candle for the Deva," humans can supposedly begin "the process of cooperation and attunement," ultimately leading to the actual clean-up of environmental pollution. They don't explain precisely how this occurs, but insist that recruits "ask inwardly for the change we'd like to see happen—such as fertility returning to a barren area or a polluted stream or toxic dump clearing up."

It is certainly newsworthy that the head of the U.N.'s environmental program endorsed such a book. It would certainly save a lot of money if these environmental clean-up methods worked as advertised. However, while there is no evidence that these thoughts alone can alter the course of nature, the possibility has to be entertained that McLaughlin and Davidson and their associates are coming into contact with something. It is significant that, in their book, they make much of the governmental research into "psychic warfare" that was referred to earlier. "The potential of the mind is tremendous," they say.

In a similar vein, Hindu meditator Sri Chimnoy, described as a U.N. "chaplain," has described the U.N. as "the way of oneness" that "leads us to the Supreme Oneness." He adds:

> The United Nations becomes for us the answer to world suffering, world darkness and world ignorance. The inner vision of the United Nations is the gift supreme. This vision the world can deny for 10, 20, 30, 40, 100 years. But a day will dawn when the vision of the United Nations will save the world. And when the reality of the United Nations starts bearing fruit, then the breath of immortality will be a living reality on Earth.[9]

There is evidence to suggest that what McLaughlin and Davidson say about this "spiritual government" may, in fact, be true. World Goodwill has written about something called "The Group of Reflection," described as "members of the U.N. Secretariat, scholars, NGOs and religious leaders." No names were provided, however. In a document, this group discussed the "intrinsic goodness" of man and declared that "the spiritual dimension" of humanity "needs to be included forthrightly in United Nations documents and activities."

Another organization working closely with the U.N. is the Temple of Understanding, explicitly dedicated to achieving "a spiritual United Nations." It has an impressive international board of advisors, board of directors, council of trustees, and council of advisors representing most religious groups.

The Temple, which maintains a "UN liaison," describes its purpose as "the worldwide promotion of interfaith dialogue and education, to achieve understanding and harmony among the people of the world's religions and beyond." However, the inclusion of controversial liberal theologian Dr. Harvey Cox on the organization's council of trustees cannot promote much harmony or understanding among those who take Christianity seriously. A long-time writer for *Playboy* magazine, he authored one article, "For Christ's Sake," containing outrageous speculation about Jesus's relationship with women and calling for the end to His portrayal as a "first century teetotaling Myra Breckinridge."

When the Temple was launched back in 1963, plans were to have an actual "temple," a $5 million futuristic building to honor the world's religions. Sponsors included John D. Rockefeller IV; Robert S. McNamara, secretary of defense in the Johnson administration, who later became head of the World Bank; and Eleanor Roosevelt, who founded the group that became known as the United Nations Association. Other endorsers included J.B. Rhine of Duke University, a researcher into paranormal activities, and Roland Gammon of the World Parliament of Religions.

The "temple" is actually going to be a "Peace Pyramid," located in the Washington, D.C. area. A proposed structure will be built on three levels symbolizing spirit, mind, and body. One level will feature a hologram of the earth, another will feature a meditation space, and the other cultural arts.

During U.N. Week in October of 1995, the fiftieth anniversary of the world body, the Temple sponsored an interfaith celebration at the Cathedral of St. John the Divine, which was described as "the official UN 50th anniversary celebration for the City of New York."

If the Reverend Pat Robertson had been part of any "official" festivities in New York, the outcry would have been deafening. But, because it involves the U.N., it's all right. And yet, the U.N. is as "religious" as any of the conservative-oriented religious groups that get regularly denounced by the liberal media as the "Christian Right." The difference is that the U.N.'s religion meshes well with radical environmentalism.

The "Temple of Understanding" provides more evidence of this fact. The group's fall 1995 newsletter included an article by Carina Courtright, a member of its board of directors, who was identified as head of a corporation "dedicated to preservation and presentation of spiritual and environmental values."

It works closely with the Cathedral of St. John the Divine, the headquarters for the Gaia Institute and the organization behind the Joint Appeal by Religion and Science for the Environment, a document issued in 1992 by 150 religious heads and scientists. One of the signers was Dr. Jessica Tuchman Mathews, then a vice-president with World Resources Institute, who became a senior fellow with the Council on Foreign Relations and a columnist for the *Washington Post*. Mathews is a major advocate of global taxes for the U.N. Another signer was Rev. Joan Campbell, general secretary of the National Council of Churches of Christ (NCC). Her involvement also carries a lot of significance.

The NCC, once known as the Federal Council of Churches, and the United Methodist church "played a crucial role in supporting the fledgling United Nations both during its creation and during the postwar years."[10] The NCC includes thirty-two Protestant and Orthodox member congregations, to which forty-nine million people belong.

During the U.N. fiftieth anniversary meetings in New York, Cuban Communist dictator Fidel Castro was happily received by one hundred church leaders convened by the Interreligious Foundation for Community Organization and the Reverend Dr. Joan Brown Campbell. Castro is a figure who "expelled most priests and nuns, closed Catholic schools and banned Christmas" after he took power.[11]

After the meeting with Castro, the Reverend Dr. Campbell praised the Communist dictator for supposedly improving the situation of the Cuban churches. "The churches now are able to carry out all the work of the church, that is the training of pastors, Sunday school teaching, evangelism and service to the society," she said.[12] But, one expert said this was demonstrably false, that "state repression" continues to exist. He said,

> The government refuses building permits for the rapidly growing church and then imprisons pastors who resort to ministering in illegal "house churches." Cuban churches cannot run schools and have no regular access to television, radio or other mass media. Missionary activity is mostly underground, and the distribution of religious literature is tightly controlled. . . . All the other adjuncts of religious freedom—freedom of expression, freedom of association, freedom of movement, freedom of the press and due process of law—are denied as well.[13]

NCC General Secretary Campbell served as executive director of the Washington office of the World Council of Churches (WCC), which has itself been accused of collaborating with the persecutors of Christians. For example, the WCC participated in a 1994 conference on "interreligious dialogue" in Sudan, where the regime is imposing Islamic law on its Christian population and "is engaged in a genocidal war with the predominantly Christian and animist population in the south."[14] Furthermore, "Sudan was reliably accused before the UN Human Rights Commission last year of having crucified Christian opponents."[15]

Paul Marshall, a professor of political theory at the Institute for Christian Studies, says it appears the WCC is following the pattern it established during the Cold War when it "engaged in long and destructive 'dialogue' with 'religious figures' from the old Communist bloc, many of whom turned out to be government agents who used these efforts as a cover to intensify persecution of the church."[16]

If the WCC was wrong about the Communists and was used by them, is it not possible that these religious figures are also seriously misguided about both the U.N. and environmental religion? In addition, as Representative Chenoweth warned, isn't persecution of "non-believers" a danger as well?

As Castro's Cuba shows, old-fashioned persecution of Christians is still occurring worldwide, and the U.N. has essentially turned a blind eye and a deaf ear to it, even though David Barrett of the World Christian Encyclopedia estimates that 160,000 Christians are killed by governments or mobs each year because of their religious identity.

Rep. Chris Smith, as chairman of the House Subcommittee on International Operations and Human Rights, held a hearing on the subject on 15 February 1996. One witness was Albert M. Pennybacker, associate general secretary of the NCC, who admitted the problem exists and said it was "appropriate" for the U.S. government to address the topic. However, as a solution, he urged "a continuing and strong commitment" to two U.N. documents, the International Covenant on Civil and Political Rights and the Declaration on the Elimination of all forms of Intolerance Based on Religion or Beliefs.

The fact is that the U.N. doesn't regard persecution of Christians to be a serious issue, as evidenced by the continuing failure of the U.N. Human Rights Commission to even mildly criticize Communist China for its massive human rights violations. Persecution of Christians, especially Catholics, is very intense in China. The panel's vote on 23 April 1996 marked the sixth year in a row that China had averted censure over its record. This time the vote was twenty-seven countries against criticizing China, twenty in favor, and six abstaining. When China won the vote, delegates "burst into applause," according to one report.

Despite this record, the NCC is still a major player in a religious lobby to strengthen the U.N. Reverend Dr. Campbell was a featured speaker at the September 1995 National Assembly on the United States and the United Nations, whose purpose was to expand the power and influence of the U.N. A panel at the event was entitled "Moral, Ethical and Spiritual Values and the U.N.," featuring Jane Blewett of the Earth Community Center, William Collins of the Baha'i Faith, Erik Larson of Brahma Kumaris, Janes Evans of Women of Reformed Judaism, and J. Philip Wogaman of Foundry United Methodist Church.

Another panel, "Religious NGOs and the U.N.," featured Douglas Hunt of the United Church of Christ Central Atlantic Conference, Betty Golomb of

Women of Reformed Judaism, Jo Marie Griesgraber of the Center of Concern, Robert McClean of the United Methodist Church/General Board of Church & Society, Janice Smith of the Baha'i International Community, and William Vendley of the World Conference on Religion and Peace.

The United Methodist Board of Church and Society has been described as the largest church lobby in Washington, D.C. and is the political arm of America's third largest religious body.

The involvement of the Roman Catholic church in these efforts is a matter of controversy and dispute. It's true that the U.S. Catholic Conference (USCC) itself has a strong pro-U.N. element and distributes two books on U.N.-related issues. For many years, the USCC was represented by Father J. Bryan Hehir, an "internationalist" who has shown a "preference for supranational forms of government." In 1983, as secretary of the USCC, he was invited by the far Left Institute for Policy Studies to deliver a lecture entitled "Matthew, Marx, Luke and John."[17]

Also within the church there is a movement, known as Liberation Theology, which historically collaborates with international communism. This movement includes former Haitian President and Catholic Priest Jean Bertrand Aristide, who was kicked out of his Catholic order for preaching violence and hatred. When Aristide was overthrown by a military group in 1991, the Vatican was the only state in the world to recognize the new anti-Aristide government. In a direct affront to the Vatican, he was restored to power by the Clinton administration and the U.N.

Robert Muller, a former assistant secretary general of the U.N. who claims to have been "personally involved" in the creation of eleven U.N. agencies and programs, has been described as a one-time Catholic who has been in contact with a number of popes. Today, however, he is described as a "visionary" who promotes the New Age movement. He envisions the U.N. as becoming "the body of Christ" and says that we should "display the U.N. flag in all houses of worship."[18]

In an interview with World Goodwill, Muller went into more detail about the spiritual dimensions of the U.N., saying, "Year after year I increase my respect for the United Nations, to the point that I consider it now as one of the greatest institutions ever created by humans, a true meta-organism for the evolution of the human species and the planet. . . . The U.N. is humanity's incipient global brain. . . . We still need a global soul, namely our consciousness and fusion with the entire universe and stream of time."

Other visionaries, considered authentic by many traditional Catholics, see the U.N. much differently. Catholic visionary Josyp Terelya, in a message some Catholics believe came from the Mother of Jesus on 18 September 1992, said:

> It is Satan himself who speaks through the false prophet of the organization of the United Nations, using the corpse of the organization . . . to deceive mankind. So it was when the forces of Satan used the League of Nations to deceive the peoples before [World War II]. And so it is today. Now understand that the devil uses invisible evil spirits, who act upon visible servants throughout the world, who are mustering the nations of the world for a world war . . . which the Lord calls the battle of the great day.[19]

Terelya went on to say that the U.N "was established through the agency of the devil, that through this diabolic exchange he might change God's kingdom into a kingdom of darkness. The devil is now using the Organization of the United Nations to deceive and to blind the nations before God's truth, to keep people from placing their trust in the Kingdom of God, which alone is the hope of the world."[20]

Another Catholic visionary, Zdenko "Jim" Singer, claiming to relay a message from Christ Himself, said:

> Nations prostitute themselves in the United Nations and My children continue to pay homage to this dead head which now lives again in that city by the ocean. Know that it is the "X," Satan's own servants who toil tirelessly to deliver My children into his clutches. Just as they contaminate and poison so much in your lives, they are the ones also overseeing the aims of that organization [the U.N.]."[21]

What happens to the Roman Catholic church and the world after the passing of Pope John Paul II is a matter of grave conjecture. Writing in *Signs of the Times* magazine, a traditional Catholic publication, Bernard and Catherine Lawrence contend that Pope John Paul II is "the last authentic Pope of these times" and that, "upon his death, the Antichrist will begin his reign."[22]

The divisions within the Roman Catholic church are real and ominous. These conflicts, however, are apparent in politics as well as religion. God's role in these unfolding developments is something beyond our absolute knowledge. As human beings exercising personal freedom, our role has to be to save ourselves through faith, with God's help, and save our families and our nation.

In this context, the evidence is unmistakable: the U.N. is an impediment to the human freedoms that God gave us. But, one doesn't have to be religious to recognize this fact. Politically, awareness is also growing. More than a half-dozen pieces of legislation were introduced in congress to restrict U.N. influence over U.S. affairs. These bills targeted U.N. taxation schemes, U.N. jurisdiction over public and private lands, U.N. control of our troops, and U.N. disarmament schemes leaving America defenseless.

Ultimately, of course, our future rests with the next generation, which must be taught the American history many of us never learned in school. By understanding the past, we can safeguard the future—a future without the U.N.

Endnotes

1. "The United Nations: Entering the Global Age," *World Goodwill Commentary* (October 1981).

2. "The New Group of World Servers," World Goodwill.

3. Russell Chandler, *Understanding the New Age* (Grand Rapids: MI.: Zondervan Publishing House, 1991), 32.

4. Michael G. Zey, *Seizing the Future* (New York: Simon & Schuster, 1994), 311.

5. *Spiritual Politics, Changing the World from the Inside Out*, flier for the book.

6. William Norman Grigg, *Freedom on the Altar. The UN's Crusade against God & Family* (Appleton, Wisconsin: American Opinion Publishing, 1995), 159.

7. Corinne McLaughlin and Gordon Davidson, *Spiritual Politics, Changing the World from the Inside Out* (New York: Ballantine Books, 1994), 318.

8. Ibid.

9. Ibid., Chandler, 185.

10. *A Global Affair, An Inside Look at the United Nations* (New York: Jones and Janello, 1995), 279.

11. Jose de Cordoba, "Bold Cuban Priest Finds Few Friends in Church or State," *Wall Street Journal*, 14 November 1995, 1.

12. "End Embargo Against Cuba, Agree Castro, U.S. Church Leaders," news release, National Council of the Churches of Christ in the USA, 26 October 1995.

13. Paul Marshall, "National Council of Churches SoftPedals Cuban Religious Persecution," *World Perspectives*, News Network International Syndicate, 17 November 1995.

14. Paul Marshall, "The WCC and the Muslims," *Faith and Freedom, The Institute on Religion and Democracy* (Spring 1995): 10.

15. Ibid.

16. Paul Marshall, "The WCC and the Muslims. Dialoguing with the Persecutors of the Church," *Faith and Freedom, Institute on Religion and Democracy* (Spring 1996).

17. "Moving the Catholic Church Leftward," The Council for the Defense of Freedom, Washington, D.C., June 1989.

18. Dennis Laurence Cuddy, Ph.D, *New is the Dawning of the New Age World Order* (Oklahoma City: Hearthstone Publishing, 1991), 271–272.

19. "Message From the Blessed Mother to Josyp Terelya," 18 September 1992, *Signs of the Times* (May/June/July 1993).

20. Ted and Maureen Flynn, *The Thunder of Justice* (Sterling, Virginia: MaxKol Communications, 1993), 289.

21. *Use My Gifts, The Messages of Our Lord*, received, documented and translated into English by Jim Z. Singer (Toronto, Canada: Ave Maria Centre of Peace, 1993), 53

22. Bernard and Catherine Lawrence, "AntiChrist Ruler of the New World Order," *Signs of Our Times* (First Quarter 1995): 46–47.